M000207393

VISUAL
THINKING
STRATEGIES
FOR PRESCHOOL

PHILIP YENAWINE

VISUAL THINKING STRATEGIES

FOR PRESCHOOL

USING ART TO ENHANCE LITERACY AND SOCIAL SKILLS

HARVARD EDUCATION PRESS
Cambridge, Massachusetts

Copyright © 2018 by the President and Fellows of Harvard College

All rights reserved. No part of this publication may be reproduced or transmitted in any form or by any means, electronic or mechanical, including photocopy, recording, or any information storage and retrieval systems, without permission in writing from the publisher.

Paperback ISBN 978-1-68253-157-0
Library Edition ISBN 978-1-68253-158-7

Library of Congress Cataloging-in-Publication Data
Names: Yenawine, Philip, author.
Title: Visual thinking strategies for preschool : using art to enhance
   literacy and social skills / Philip Yenawine.
Description: Cambridge, Massachusetts : Harvard Education Press, 2018. |
   Includes bibliographical references and index.
Identifiers: LCCN 2017055264| ISBN 9781682531570 (pbk.) |
   ISBN 9781682531587 (library edition)
Subjects: LCSH: Art appreciation--Study and teaching (Primary) |
   Visualization. | Critical thinking. | Meaning (Psychology) | Metacognition
   in children. | Early childhood education. | Children--Language.
Classification: LCC N361 .Y46 2018 | DDC 701/.18--dc23 LC record available
   at https://lccn.loc.gov/2017055264

Published by Harvard Education Press,
an imprint of the Harvard Education Publishing Group

Harvard Education Press
8 Story Street
Cambridge, MA 02138

Cover Design: Endpaper Studio
Cover Image: Ekely/DigitalVision Vectors/Getty Images
The typefaces used in this book are Berkeley Old Style, and ITC Legacy Sans.

CONTENTS

INTRODUCTION

FOR THOSE OF US lucky enough to have grandchildren who figure prominently in our lives, moments that take our breath away are common. As I watched my three-year-old granddaughter spend some of her post-nap burst of energy jumping up and down on a miniature trampoline, with a grin that goes from ear to ear, I chuckled with my own delight. She moves with obvious excitement at being able to jump with abandon, knowing that a balance bar will keep her steady for the split seconds that her stockinged feet leave the surface. Jumping for the joy of it. It must feel pretty close to flying.

This isn't going to sound right, but frankly I experience just as much pleasure from being told, as she looked at the food on her plate a few minutes later, "I don't like Brussels sprouts." I am delighted because only a few short months ago she might have simply pushed them away when her mom put them in front of her. The full sentences that now emerge regularly as part of our conversations—despite occasional needs for interpretation—are part of the marvel of children this age. "A great miracle in childhood is the emergence of language without explicit instruction" is the way that child speech pathologist Diane Zimmerman puts it.[1]

The part of early language development that I've known since my own children were tiny was the fact that adults in the lives of little ones have a responsibility to talk to kids about what they see and do, read to them, discuss what's going on, ask them questions, listen, and try to make sense of their early attempts at talking. What I needed to get through my head, however, was the child's job in what is actually a two-way street. Yes, children need to hear language, but every bit as

1

much, they need to engage in verbal give-and-take as soon as they start to babble.

Language doesn't simply happen. It's the result of many things and perhaps most important is a child's verbal interactions with older people and other children. Research tells us that the more verbal exchanges among toddlers and others, the greater their ease and success with language in the long run, though a proviso is that the exchanges need to be positive. "Don't do that" doesn't really count. Children learn to speak by talking with others—from communicating, not just from hearing words or commands. In the absence of dialogue, language development is slowed, and in the view of some, irrevocably.

For me, the decision to write this book about Visual Thinking Strategies (VTS) for children from three to five has a great deal to do with making sure that all children have a chance at meaningful verbal give-and-take. By the time children start preschool, most have some ability to talk, but one of the key arguments for universal preschool is to make sure that regardless of their skill level as they enter, all know the basics of communication by the time they head to kindergarten. VTS can help ensure that growth: kids talk about what they see in pictures, assisted by teachers. The pictures are artworks carefully chosen to connect to the life experiences of the children and as such provide much for the children to observe, consider, and talk about. The painting by Francisco de Goya[2] in figure I.1 has had wonderful responses from young children over many years. You might examine it to see why you think this has been the case.

The discussions resonate to the point that VTS has proved to be a useful and gratifying addition to teachers' tools for building language. For example, Dori Jacobsohn, who trains teachers in early childhood instruction including VTS, heard from teachers in Detroit that the impact produced more "productive talk" throughout the day.[3]

One challenge for educators in general is maintaining a fruitful balance of talking to young people, letting them talk, helping them listen, expanding their exposure to what's around them, and introducing new

FIGURE I.1   Francisco José de Goya y Lucientes, *The Seesaw*

language and information when it's wanted and needed. When these strands are woven together into experience that feels real, useful, and authentic—and the less likely it feels like rote exercise—the greater the likelihood that the children learn in ways that stick. VTS for preschool is designed to do just this.

In the following chapters, teachers talk about what we have learned from watching three- and four-year-olds focus on a series of well-chosen images and talk themselves into understanding what they see in response to four short, carefully designed questions. Teachers are, in fact, the people who convinced me that VTS might be something valued in early education though it took several years for me to get comfortable with this concept. I should have been more open to begin with because anyone like me who's spent time with young children knows images are important to them. Simply looking at things holds their attention longer than it does for most of us. Their literature is full of illustrations for reasons. Drawing is equally important: given materials, most children take great pleasure in making images beginning with scribbles. But all that said, I didn't see how these behaviors might argue in favor of assembling preschool kids into groups, sitting them on the floor, and asking them to discuss what they saw in pictures.

WHERE VTS COMES FROM

VTS evolved over more than a dozen years of field research to see if and how it worked—what teachers and students experienced, how teachers used it, and what growth it produced. Cognitive psychologist Abigail Housen and I led the team, and this process involved many schools that let their classrooms become laboratories. That work is described in a book that is essentially a companion to this, *Visual Thinking Strategies: Using Art to Deepen Learning Across School Disciplines.*[4] But here's the short history.

When we first drafted VTS in 1991, I was director of education at the Museum of Modern Art in New York. Housen and I hoped the teaching would jump-start skills that museum visitors thought they lacked, limiting their pleasure looking at art. We tested our new lessons in schools to get some sense of their impact; teachers were willing to let us collect data from students over time, which is hard to do in museums because visits are usually occasional, informal, and infrequent.

In the earliest days of experimenting with ways to build observation skills and rapport with art, Housen and I, with help from others, concentrated our research on testing with fifth graders and their teachers. In 1991, grade 5 was typically the highest grade in elementary schools, and given that it was slightly before the era of pervasive standardized curricula and testing, teachers had more time and energy to try something new. The arts, while always underfunded, remained on the radar of many schools. Meanwhile, irrepressible ten-year-olds were the perfect age and stage for lessons that asked them to look at carefully chosen works of art and discuss what they saw in an open-ended way.

Given our intention to build viewing skills—another way of saying "visual literacy"—we had data to help us start the learning. Abigail Housen had been studying how people think when looking at art for over fifteen years. We had her data about how the brain processed observations while looking at art—and how the cognition changed as experience grew—to help us start. We used this information as the basis for creating lessons that enabled elementary students to use existing skills—the ability to observe, to talk, and to make sense of observations, for example—to start the teaching/learning, and then to increase the skills involved in finding meaning in the array of images that surround us in the modern world. We watched and documented what happened and folded what we learned into extensions of the original lessons as well as into the frequent revisions we did based on what we continued to learn. Many of us watch VTS in practice to this day to see how it works with students, if and how it affects teacher practice, and if it can be used in additional contexts.

Even the first draft of the curriculum was well received. Teachers could and would teach it and let us watch and study the process. Early data indicated that our lessons were effective in producing growth in what we called viewing skills, our initial objective. Teachers meanwhile noticed other benefits. When third- and fourth-grade teachers caught wind of an activity that seemed to engage virtually all students in fifth grade—even those who seldom raised their hands—and during which disagreements as to meaning could be discussed civilly by often-contentious classmates, they asked if they could give this approach a try as well. I was very comfortable finding images for fourth graders but a bit less so as we got to the lower grades.

Within a few years, our school data revealed that the set of lessons, taught in a roughly ten-lesson sequence, did increase particular skills: students made more observations, and these observations became more detailed and focused over time; they drew more inferences from these observations; and they backed up more opinions with evidence. Importantly, we found that the skills stuck: they remained in place when students were studied several years later, after the VTS lessons stopped. To find all this out, Housen used existing tools and protocols, both pre- and posttests—and also developed more—to document thinking and, later, language.

Our findings were good news for us in museums because careful observation and thinking deeply about what one sees are obviously germane to people looking at art. What came as a pleasant surprise was how these same skills served school priorities as well. Early reports indicated two aspects in particular, neither predicted by us. The first was that thinking skills showed up in other lessons, especially when evidence was required to back up an answer. In addition, students wrote more and better when the prompt was a work of art, beginning as early as second grade, something that teachers discovered. Teachers told us that VTS was beneficial within the larger frame of what their students were expected to accomplish academically.

Another surprise to us was the impact of discussions on social behavior. VTS discussions seemed to engage all students; for example, even students who didn't participate normally in class felt comfortable contributing ideas during VTS discussions. A second was that students could disagree with one another during VTS and not get angry about their differences. Discussions had a civility about them sometimes missing in other classroom lessons and activities. A third—not seen immediately—was the confidence children developed slowly but surely in their own voices and in the validity of their opinions.

We were, of course, delighted with reports about these social behaviors at the time, but their importance has grown as schools have assumed more responsibility for social and emotional growth of young people, not just academic achievement.

By now, VTS has a long history of usefulness in the elementary grades, and I wrote about this in *Visual Thinking Strategies: Using Art to Deepen Learning Across School Disciplines*. Despite its usefulness throughout later grades, it took me awhile to get comfortable with developing a version tailored to preschool. This book tells that story while offering guidance to preschool educators on how to use VTS.

THE ORIGINS OF VTS FOR PRESCHOOL

Enter a fearless, experienced kindergarten teacher, Debby Robin, of Urbana, Illinois. She knew VTS was worth a try with her students. The results she reported back opened my skeptical eyes to a potential I'd not seen. Children willingly grouped around the poster-sized reproductions we selected as they would for a reading group. They raised their hands and took turns. They mentioned what they noticed; those that saw something they had no language for got up and pointed to the images. At first, some repeated what others had mentioned, but over time, more of them made new discoveries to point out and name. It became clear to Debby that they were listening to one another. She wasn't surprised (even if I was), but both of us—and other veteran teachers at Debby's school—were delighted. The notion of a K–5 sequential curriculum began to take shape.

A few years later, building on what we learned from watching VTS in kindergarten, another determined educator/researcher, Paula Lynn, began experimenting with VTS discussions among groups of preschoolers. At the time (2008), Paula was working at the Isabella Stewart Gardner Museum in Boston in the museum's school partnership programs. I knew she was doing it and was once again skeptical that the most basic rigors of VTS—sitting and looking in a group, taking turns, speaking—would be too challenging for the developmental levels of children as young as two and a half to four. Again, Paula showed me potential I'd not foreseen. I made an unfortunately common error: underestimating children.

Paula wrote me recently describing her experience back then. It wasn't smooth sailing all the way, but instead a process full of discoveries.

I quickly realized that the students needed to hone their communication skills if we were to have constructive discussions together. It is developmentally appropriate for children this young to be focused on the self; they operate in a space that is their own and what others do or say rarely has an impact on what they will do or say next. For example, multiple students may point out the same tree because unless they themselves have said it, it's as if it has not been said. The fact that many of these children didn't speak English might have had an impact on this. Knowing that, patience was paramount.

It was a little more than half way through the year before I started to notice their collective growth in being able to communicate effectively within a group. That included listening, taking turns, raising their hand to share, elaborating on their ideas, and even referencing other comments by using classmates' names. I remember an instance towards the end of the year when a boy was sharing what he saw in a painting by building on what another student mentioned. He began by saying, "That's a rocking chair . . . like she said." The girl he was referring to turned her head towards him and said, "I have a name!" It was both a humorous and pivotal moment. The students were becoming aware of the fact that during our discussions we respected others by using their name.[5]

The most surprising result of Paula's carefully observed practice was that in time many children would not simply see and name things they saw, but they inferred meanings beyond simple observations—"I think she's eating," for example. While that was delightful news, what truly astonished me was that a significant number of them could, when asked, identify what they saw that led them to a particular conclusion— "Because she's standing by a table." Given the right images, a strategy that worked in the early grades (K–2) was effective in preschool.

With Paula putting wind into my sails, and again with the help of both VTS colleagues and preschool teachers, VTS for preschool took the shape I share with you in this book. The adaptations are significant though relatively modest. The basic premise remains the same: give children a chance to draw on their ample ability to look, make sense of what they see, and express their responses in a structured way.

VTS image discussions require what children are great at—learning from what they see. We chose to base the discussions on visual art because it's a particularly rich form of imagery, one that begs viewers of any age to explore deeply and to probe beyond first impressions. We initiate and extend the process using open-ended questions that enable kids to mine images for whatever stories are meaningful to them. We facilitate the process by listening and supporting children's comments and helping them enjoy the game of figuring out meanings together.

VTS IN PRESCHOOL: THE ADAPTATIONS

Word regarding VTS in preschool began to get out. With the enthusiasm of people ready for a new opportunity, my colleagues and I began responding to requests from preschool teachers to give VTS a try. Importantly, we found sites willing to let us join them as they watched to see both teacher and student change over a multiyear period. In what follows, you'll read what we have learned, and you'll meet some of the remarkable people who showed us the way. To write this book, I have pulled together the thoughts of trainers, teachers, school directors, and my own observations from multiple years of implementing VTS in preschools in many parts of this country and in different types of schools.

The impact of VTS on children in preschool is still unfolding; what's established clearly is that it becomes a teacher's trusted companion in efforts to build children's willingness to express themselves orally, gain confidence, and have a sense of their own points of view as well as their interest in hearing the ideas of others. They make more observations and infer more meaning from them, both having an impact on language. A more general impact is that VTS experience gives children tools for making sense of much that was previously unfamiliar, skills that transcend VTS discussions, enabling exploration of many subjects and phenomena at school and at home. And, of course, children begin to view art with comfort, a win for anyone who cares about developing visual literacy alongside verbal literacy.

As it has developed, the key differences between VTS for preschool and for older students lie in

- the choices of images: they are simpler, more tailored to predictable life experiences of any given group of students, as in more city images for city kids.
- the duration of lessons: discussions are shorter (usually eight to twelve minutes instead of fifteen to twenty in K–5), usually focusing on one image at a time.

- the numbers of discussions over time: there is no limit; teachers are encouraged to conduct as many as they see helpful, usually between ten and twenty over the year.
- the phrasing of the opening questions: we add both "What do you see in this picture?" and "What do you notice here?" to the basic set that starts with "What's going on in this picture?" and "What more can you find?"
- the timing of introducing an additional question asking for evidence, specifically "What do you see that makes you say that?" For preschool, we ask teachers to watch for the time when it seems developmentally appropriate to challenge students to add reasons for thinking something.
- the expectations of behavior: teachers in preschool allow more flexibility, for example, letting children walk up to point to what they are talking about in an image if that's needed—and it sometimes is.

Teachers also expect more subjective ideas from the kids based on their necessarily limited experience (they haven't been around all that long) and often in highly personal ways. It therefore takes more reading between the lines to understand precisely what children are thinking and talking about in order to paraphrase their comments, a key aspect of facilitating discussions. (VTS for preschool is described in detail in chapter 2.)

THE PURPOSE OF THIS BOOK

My intention with this book is to equip early childhood educators and others to try VTS with young people in their lives!

The movement toward universal preschool is part of the reason for the urgency of this book. As curricula for early childhood are still somewhat in flux, we need to think of what gives children the best foundation for later schooling and for life. Pressure exists to start academics early, and it's both my strongly held view that this is a mistake and this opinion is shared by more and more people studying the impact of preschool on later achievement.

During these tender but enormously fertile years, children need nurture more than academic rigor. They need to be helped to learn by dint of their own efforts, not only by direction from others. They need to go from following their noses to directing their attention. They need more time with creative play and active exploration aided by teachers with questions and suggestions more than directions. They need to create and solve their own problems independently with help only as needed. They need to be supervised but not always told what, when, and how to behave. They need to figure out how to share and engage with others by seeing behavior modeled in relevant circumstances, not just by being taught rules to follow. They need experience with real-life challenges and activities, ones whose inherent usefulness is obvious to them. They need to learn language by way of authentic communication, not rote memorization.

Decades of research and theory back up this thinking, and whole methods such as Montessori and Reggio Emilia exist as examples to guide the kind of teaching that produces empowered, capable, confident, and creative learners as a result of preschool. VTS as an activity fits within child-centered perimeters and greatly assists meeting these objectives.

In the succeeding chapters, I illustrate VTS in operation with groups of children at different points in their VTS experience, providing you with a picture of what a teacher does and what students do in response. I explain each element in the teaching strategy with comments from teachers to help illustrate their understandings of them. I detail what we know about the impact of VTS discussions on student learning, and later, what teachers discover about this additional way of teaching, more facilitative than directive and more open ended than many are used to. When I think it might be useful, I provide summary notes and tips at the ends of chapters to make it easier for you to put VTS into practice.

VTS is a structured activity that allows for independent and authentic observation, thinking, and expression, supported actively by teachers. I hope you're intrigued enough to get started with kids in your life!

CHAPTER 1

VTS in Preschool

What Does It Look Like?

LET'S JUMP RIGHT INTO taking a look at VTS in operation. I want to start by sharing part of a discussion among students who were totally new to VTS. This discussion is borrowed from a blog post by Chicago-based early childhood specialist Dori Jacobsohn, who trains others to use VTS in preschool.[1] These four-year-olds were examining a Pablo Picasso painting entitled *Child with a Dove* (see figure 1.1).[2] Because this was their first such discussion, they were unfamiliar with the process. (I've used pseudonyms throughout all discussions in this book to protect the children.)

As usual, the students were given a few moments to look at the image in silence before Dori asked the first question:

DORI: *What's happening in this picture?*
ADAM: *There's a boy.*
DORI: *You're noticing this figure in the center, and you're thinking it might be boy. What do you see that makes you say it's a boy?*
ADAM: *Boys have hair like that.*
DORI: *So you're noticing the hairstyle and it reminds you of the way a boy might wear his hair. What more can we find?*
BELLA: *Uh ah, it's a girl!*
DORI: *Bella has another idea about the child and she thinks it might be a girl.*
BELLA: *No, it IS a girl!*

FIGURE 1.1   Pablo Picasso, *Child with a Dove*

DORI: *Bella, what do you see that is making you say, "Girl"?*

BELLA: *She has a dress.*

DORI: *So the outfit is your clue and it reminds you of a girl's dress. What more can we find?*

BELLA: *It is!*

DORI: *Marta, I see your hand is up. What's happening here?*

Marta walks over to the image and points at the ball, and smiles at Dori.

DORI: *Marta noticed something not mentioned before—that there is a ball near the bottom left of the picture. What more can we find in this image? Jon, what more?*

JON: *Zoe is a girl and she has short hair.*

DORI: *You've been thinking hard about this person and noticed Zoe sitting next to you wears her hair short, so perhaps it's a girl. Pieter, I see your hand up. What more can you find?*

PIETER: *Those are boy shoes. It's a boy.*

DORI: *We have a different clue from the clothes. Bella thinks it's a girl because of the dress, and you noticed the style of shoes and speculate it might be a boy. We have a few different ideas about who this child might be. What more can we find, Junie?*

JUNIE: *What's she holding?*

DORI: *Junie is looking at another part of the picture and wondering what this might be?* (Dori points to an object in figure's hands.)

And so it continued. The total discussion lasted approximately fifteen minutes, a fairly long time; typically, conversations go from ten to twelve minutes. VTS conversations in preschool focus on one image, as is the case both here and in the later discussions cited.

What can we learn from quick analysis of this discussion? Although the process was new to them, the children seemed to understand what was asked from the start: to look and to talk about what they saw. They began to make observations. The first of these, "It's a boy," might seem a straightforward observation, but Dori actually thought the child inferred something about the figure, its gender. So she asked a question, "What do you see that makes you say this is a boy?" The question asked the child to look again at the picture and find visual evidence to back up his comment, and he did so: the figure's hair. Phrased the way the question was, the task of supplying evidence didn't seem hard at all for this four-year-old.

This response, however, didn't sit well with the next child, who drew a different inference from the same figure. "It's a girl!" asserted Bella, who was clearly paying attention to Dori and emphatically objected to Dori's characterization of the comment, "It *might be* a girl." No, the dress means it's a girl, for sure!

The next child changed the subject, maybe breaking the tension. Marta, who was likely less comfortable speaking (perhaps English was her second language), walked up to the reproduction and pointed to something new. Dori saw that she was interested in a ball in the painting's foreground, and named it to make it clear to everyone, perhaps especially to Marta, that she understood what the child saw and that there is a word for it. Since Marta's contribution seemed a straightforward observation, Dori moved on by asking one other question of the whole group, "What more can we find?"

The next two comments sent us back into the disputed gender territory: both hairstyles and shoes are familiar indicators of gender to the children. Dori helped them understand the diversity of opinion by stressing that, "We have a few different ideas about who this child might be." In other words, she anticipated a direction the discussion seemed to be headed by referring to the differences of opinion; we call this "linking." It can be used to indicate that we have a diversity of opinions, as here, or equally effectively by linking points of agreement.

When Dori reopened the discussion by asking, "What more can we find?" Junie changed the subject again, asking a question about what the child is holding. This was not the end of the discussion. It carried on for another ten minutes as the students continued to make new observations as well as debate ideas already expressed.

Part of the credit for the children's extended focus, thoughtful comments, and orderly discussion goes to Dori, of course, a veteran with regard to preschool as well as VTS. Clearly, the children were comfortable with her.

Another factor at work here is that the task seemed to suit the children perfectly. I wasn't always sure it would. As with VTS in the older grades, VTS for preschool involves showing students carefully selected works of art and asking them to talk about what they see—in other words, participate in discussions. The process is driven by a set of open-ended questions—first, "What's going on (or happening) in this picture?" (or "What do you see?" Or "What do you notice in this picture?"). After opening comments are made in response to the first question, another is introduced: "What more can we find?"

Teachers listen carefully to what children mention, point to each observation, and respond to students by paraphrasing each child's thoughts. When appropriate, teachers ask another question: "What do you see that makes you say that?" It initially seemed that this was a lot to ask of four-year-olds. You can judge for yourself whether or not my reservations were reasonable by reading on.

A MIDYEAR DISCUSSION

Toward the close of a busy morning in her preK classroom, Sarah O'Leary assembled her lively four-year-olds on the rug used for meetings, reading, and other group activities. With the kids sitting around the perimeter, Sarah asked them to look at a poster-sized reproduction of a painting for a moment without talking. She broke the silence by asking a question, "What's going on in this picture?" and the children's eagerness to answer was obvious. Everyone seemed to have something to say.

I was visiting Sarah and her students one crisp, clear morning in January at a school in the heart of Boston's Chinatown, and the children had been discussing pictures in this way since the beginning of the year. Students knew the drill: answer the questions by mentioning things they notice in the picture. All remained engaged for over ten minutes of sharing ideas before Sarah brought the discussion to an end, just in time for lunch. I stood nearby watching the process. There were no issues keeping them on their bums as they focused for the entire time.

Sarah routinely uses her cellphone to videotape activities in the classroom so that she can look at and discuss what happens with her assistant teacher. We too can therefore look in on a VTS lesson that took place about a month before my visit. I transcribed the students' comments and interactions with Sarah.[3] The painting they examined was by Horace Pippin and entitled *Domino Players* (see figure 1.2).[4] It's going to be helpful for you to take a good look at the picture before reading on, something we ask the kids to do as well.

Sarah started by showing students the laminated poster of Pippin's painting. She quickly asked them to look at it in silence. "Take a moment to look at this artwork," she instructed the kids. "Take time to look from top to bottom, from left to right, at big details and small details. Put your thumbs over your heart if you see something," her alternative to raising hands to get them used to take turns. Meanwhile, she surveyed the group attentively. At one point she said, "I love that you are still looking and showing focus." When she sensed it was time, she asked the opening question and started calling on students one at a time but naming others who would get the next turns.

SARAH: *Rosie, what's going on in this artwork?*

ROSIE: *They are eating.*

SARAH: *Are you referring to this group of people in the middle? Do you remember that in last week's picture we thought some people might be cutting food? So Rosie thinks these people might be eating.* (As the child spoke, Sarah pointed to the people at the table, and she continued to point throughout the discussion.)

SARAH: *What more can we find? Tamara?*

TAMARA: *It looks like, um, the people, um, I think they are, um, cutting flowers.*

FIGURE 1.2   Horace Pippin, *Domino Players*

SARAH: *Ah! So you have a different idea. Rosie thought they might be eating food, but you think they . . . maybe they are cutting flowers. What do you see that makes you think they are cutting something?*

TAMARA: *Because they have to cut flowers to keep them growing.*

SARAH: *So you are thinking that they . . . maybe they would have to cut the flowers to keep them growing. Taipai, what more can we find?*

TAIPAI: *I see the red thing.*

SARAH: *Are you looking down here at the bottom?*

TAIPAI: *Yes.*

SARAH: *Okay, Taipai is seeing something red here on the bottom. Taipai, can you say anything more?*

TAIPAI: *I see scissors.*

SARAH: *Oh, so Tamara thought the people might be cutting something and Taipai sees some scissors down here on the bottom and she sees some red. Let's have some more thumbs up. Leilia, what more can we find?*

LEILIA: *I see a crown.*

SARAH: *Are you looking on the right, or the middle, or the left? Can you come up and show me?* (Because Sarah didn't recognize what Leilia saw as a crown, Leilia came to the image, pointed to the top of the glass globe on the lamp at the upper right of the painting. Other children came up, or tried to, when they struggled with words though Sarah always asked them to use their words first, as you will notice.)

SARAH: *Leilia is noticing a shape up here near the top. Leilia, what do you see that makes you think this shape is a crown?*

LEILIA: *Because it has one, two, three, four points.*

SARAH: *Ah so, Leilia counted these pointed shapes, and it reminds her of a crown. I see many thumbs up. I'll call on all of you, but Raymond first, what more can we find?*

RAYMOND: *I see that they have some white things on.*

SARAH: *So Raymond is noticing the clothes that they're wearing and sees that the bottom part is white. Let's see. Emily, what more can we find?*

EMILY: *It looks like, um, it looks like they have a dog?*

SARAH: *Where are you looking? You may come up if you want, but try to use your words first.*

EMILY: *Next to the chair.*

SARAH: *Ah, right by where Taipai found the scissors. Emily is seeing some details and she is wondering if it might be a dog. Do you remember last week we saw a dog in the middle of the artwork we looked at then? Emily is looking and thinking we may see a dog here. Let's look some more. Nathan?*

NATHAN: *I think the people are playing checkers.*

SARAH: *Ah—so we've had a few ideas. Maybe eating food, maybe cutting flowers, but you are thinking they are playing a game. What do you see that makes you say that it's checkers?*

NATHAN: *Cause you can see the dots on them.*

SARAH: *So you remember that checkers is a game where the pieces have dots on them so you think that it might be the game checkers. Thomas, what more can we find?* (He started to get up.) *Try to use your powerful words.*

THOMAS: *I see that there are shapes up there so those could be a car.*

SARAH: *Can you show me where you mean? Can you tell me anything more?*

THOMAS: *These might be a car.*

SARAH: *Okay, thank you. Thomas is looking at the details over here on the right and what he sees reminds him of a car. What more can we find? Use your words. Eric, what do you see? I know that you're thinking.*

ERIC: *I think that's fire.*

SARAH: *So Thomas looked at these shapes and they remind him of a car, and Eric thinks that it could be a fire. Eric, what do you see that makes you say fire?*

ERIC: *Because it has these lines like those.*

SARAH: *Do you remember when Leilia was pointing near the top and she noticed these pointed lines that might make the shape of a crown? Well, Eric is noticing similar shapes here—we are seeing lots of shapes today— and because of what he's seeing in these lines, he thinks this might be fire.*

SARAH: *Thank you very much, friends. You had lots of good ideas to share today.*

After eight minutes of focused attention—very little wiggling even—they needed to stop for lunch. Sarah said that she could see that some still had things to say, so she told them to whisper their ideas to a partner. They were familiar with this process and went right to it. That did not stop a couple of irrepressible kids from calling out a couple of additional ideas, continuing to build on earlier comments, one seeing a second fire—this time in the lamp—and another thought the crown shape might be a flower. Sarah brought the activity to a close by thanking the children again for their excellent observations.

What we can see from this sample discussion is that the children readily make observations, most fairly simple. Some of these are easy for others to see (the skirts the women are wearing and the scissors, for example), and some are harder to fathom—what we describe as personal and idiosyncratic, exactly as you might expect of four-year-olds— for example, the assertion that the figures are cutting flowers. It's also pretty hard to find a dog without the child's help.

Whenever their observations were interpretations of what they saw (such as, "I see a crown, a car, or fire"), Sarah asked the follow-up question: What do you see that makes you say that? We call this the "evidence question," and it's a direct and concrete way to seek an explanation grounded in visual details from the picture. As with the original observations, some explanations are easy to follow (the jagged lines do make a shape resembling a crown, other shapes resemble fire); some not so much (again, the explanations intended to explain the flower cutting or the car).

Sarah demonstrated that she was listening to the children by pointing to what they said (or asking them to do so if she was unsure) and paraphrasing each response. She phrased her responses carefully, "Rosie thought they *might be* eating food, but you think they *may be* cutting flowers." Sarah is using what we call "conditional language," and she used it repeatedly as Dori did to Bella's dismay. This is a way of acknowledging the comment without signaling that it is true, even if the comment were spot on. The children were used to this, and Thomas even followed suit when he talked about the possibility of a car: "I see that there are shapes up there so those *could be* a car."

In this way, Sarah subtly introduced the idea that an image might contain details that can be interpreted a variety of ways, leaving room for new ideas. For example, someone could have said the figure on the right is sewing, maybe making a quilt. Or, although two of the central figures seem to be playing a game, another—the one leaning on her elbows—might only be watching.

Conditional phrasing allows for multiple stories to emerge from the same image. It is unlikely children this age will mine them all or even be conscious of the thinking behind the phrasing, but still Sarah introduced the concept little by little, and we can see that Thomas, at least, has already gotten the point.

One further aspect of Sarah's facilitation that should be noted was her use of linking to connect two comments, ones that support one another: "Tamara thought the people might be cutting something and Taipai sees some scissors down here on the bottom . . ."

When I talked to Sarah about this discussion, she told me she was delighted by how many comments dealt with shapes because they indicated that the children were very likely listening to one another, a remarkable skill for four-year-olds. Leilia's early comment about shapes—the ones that to her defined a crown—seemed to catch on, for example. Sarah helped make this happen by the way she paraphrased: "Leilia is noticing a shape up here near the top . . . Ah so, Leilia counted these pointed shapes, and it reminds her of a crown." She acknowledged Leilia's thinking by paraphrasing the salient aspect of the comment— reading shapes as describing something.

Moving along, through continuously asking "What more can we find?" Sarah left the floor open to whatever interested the children. All seemed to feel comfortable contributing thoughts—nothing they said was going to be judged either wrong or right, but for several children, finding shapes was the focus. I expected them to keep trying to find more of a storyline (as in what the people depicted might be doing) but the through line was shapes.

MORE ADVANCED DISCUSSION: CHILDREN WITH UP TO THREE YEARS' EXPERIENCE

We return to analyzing the facilitation process later, but before we go deeper, let's look at one other discussion. Both of the examples we've looked at are typical of what preschool teachers can expect with VTS within the time frame of a year. Here's another among children in a preschool that begins with toddlers—the Charlestown Nursery School, in a neighborhood within Boston, Massachusetts.[5]

Their teacher is Erika Miles, a much admired veteran early childhood educator who has been including VTS among her teaching strategies for almost five years, since it was first introduced at this remarkable school. Most of the children in this prekindergarten grouping have had VTS for two years, a few for three. The children are discussing Pablo Picasso's *Le Gourmet* (see figure 1.3).[6] Erika's facilitation has been removed to make it easier to concentrate on the children's comments. Look to see similarities and differences among these comments and

FIGURE 1.3   Pablo Picasso, *Le Gourmet*

ones from the preceding examples. The conversation began after the usual moments of silent looking, which Erika referred to as "mindful observation," in keeping with an intention of the school in general: being present in the moment.

> ANA: *There's a little girl standing up and eating her porridge. She's a girl because of her hair and dress.*
> CHARLES: *She's stirring her porridge.*
> LARA: *It looks like she doesn't have a mom or dad. Because they're not there.*
> BECCA: *It doesn't really seem like the first picture I saw.*
> WILLA: *It looks like his mom and dad are in a different place.*
> STEFAN: *Maybe the parents are behind the curtains.*
> MARNIE: *There's a ghost behind the curtains.*
> TODD: *This guy wants to get to a playground.*
> DELIA: *Maybe the mom and dad are at the other half of the table but you just can't see them.*
> SCOTT: *A rock on the table. It's a rock because it has dots.*
> DELIA: *The curtains are in the other half of the picture too.*
> ELSIE: *I've seen this picture before.*
> LUCIEN: *Maybe the mom and dad are taking a nap.*

What's new here, different from what we saw in the first two samples? Let's start with Ana's opening comment: "There's a little girl standing up and eating her porridge. She's a girl because of her hair and dress." Anyone hearing this kind of description would think, "Yeah, that makes sense," in contrast with, say, the flower-cutting description of the second example. This response includes detail that children with less experience don't mention: it's a "little" girl, eating "porridge," and two pieces of evidence—"hair and dress"—signify to Ana that the figure is a girl. Her description is given by way of a full sentence with two clauses. Taken as a whole, we might say Ana outlined essential details of a short story.

Hearing this comment, I could forgive Erika for wondering what was left for other students to find, but Charles, probably having listened to Ana, elaborated on the story: "She's stirring her porridge," again a logical conclusion given what's depicted. Lara shifted the discussion from what's there to what's missing—the parents are "not there"—initiating a new story element that appeared to interest the children for the rest of the discussion. Willa, Stefan, and Lucien also mentioned the parents and offered different explanations for the absence: the parents might be in a "different place," "behind the curtains," or "taking a nap." Delia gave this thinking a twist by introducing the table. Recognizing that we see only a part of it, she theorized the parents might be there, just sitting where we can't see them.

Meanwhile, other children felt comfort changing the subject in different ways: Becca not recognizing this image, Elsie thinking it's familiar, Marnie wondering if a ghost might hide behind the curtains, Todd projecting what the figure (to him a boy) might be wishing, and Scott pointing out a detail left out of the discussion to that point, a shape he saw as a rock with dots on the table.

Erika likely took several things away from this discussion. Some are that the children collectively can make a pretty thorough inventory of what's depicted, and they provide good description of what they see, more than they once did. Their interpretations have begun to take the shape of early storytelling, and that has implications for literacy. The children are listening to each other, but regardless of what the majority finds, Erika has made others feel comfortable contributing different perspectives. Finally, particularly given the school's emphasis on social and emotional growth alongside intellectual, she might think that missing parents, and the need to address their absence, were on the children's minds. When I asked her about this, she reported that it was something she'd thought about. She told me, "This particular class was very concerned about where the parents were when talking about this picture, and I think that is because parents are an extension of themselves at this young age and it can be a little scary to think about them not being close by."[7]

We will spend a good deal of time going over the elements of VTS in chapter 2, partly to become clear about what caused the changes we saw in the last discussion. We'll address the implications of VTS for children's growth even more in chapter 4, but for now, let's summarize what's been said about VTS: So far you know that

VTS involves discussions of images facilitated by a teacher.

A few open-ended questions drive the process.

Students are supported in their responses by teachers who listen carefully to what they say and who find a way to rephrase each idea.

Paraphrases are usually expressed in conditional language.

Disparate as well as convergent ideas are linked.

As we focus on VTS practice and get more granular—exactly what each VTS element is and what learning objectives each addresses—please keep these three discussions in mind. Keep picturing young children you know and put them in the places of the ones you've just observed. And remember that all the pictures included in the book provide guides to the sorts of images you might show your students. All are available by way of Google images and usually accompanied by others that might also be appropriately interesting and engaging.

CHAPTER 2

Key Elements of VTS Discussions

BY THE TIME YOU COMPLETE THIS BOOK, I want you to feel both motivated and capable of trying VTS yourself. This chapter explains each element of the strategy in depth. I want you to come away knowing the reasoning behind each of the consciously designed, research-driven aspects of VTS, created to help little ones negotiate the new territory of preschool and prepare for what is to come. These early years are too important for children's growth to waste a minute of their time, and VTS represents the kind of engagement that helps children discover and work up to the potential of these years.

In the pages to come, I examine each VTS element in the context of preschool. You've already encountered them as Dori, Sarah, and Erika modeled them with their classes: VTS involves discussions initiated by images; jump-started by questions; and facilitated by teachers who listen, point, paraphrase, and link in response to children's comments.

This approach seems simple enough, and on one level it is. The few questions can be memorized. That said, listening as attentively and insightfully as is required is harder than most of us think. Finding words to rephrase short, incomplete thoughts is challenging. Preschoolers' comments are sometimes hard to understand because of missing vocabulary or the quirkiness of a child's view, but they usually are pretty straightforward and concrete once you get the idea.

Getting to be good at VTS is worth the effort. VTS is perhaps more useful in preschool than in later grades, although it took me a long time to believe it would work at all. It provides a foundation for learning and language in all children in a way that helps them reach their creative and cognitive potential. How it works to do that will come to you as you get better at it and see the impact on kids. So let's get going!

THE REASON FOR DISCUSSIONS

VTS involves discussions, a chance for preschoolers to talk, sharing and debating observations and ideas in an open-ended way. Lauren Resnick and Catherine Snow get right to the point of why this is important in the preface to their practical, down-to-earth book for teachers, *Speaking and Listening for Preschool Through Third Grade*. They state, "Speaking and listening are the foundations of reading and writing. A child who does not have a large and fluent vocabulary will have difficulty with every aspect of reading, from recognizing or sounding out words to making sense of a story or set of directions. A child who can't tell a story orally will have trouble writing one."[1]

This clarity obviously speaks directly to one reason VTS is useful in preschool: giving a chance for children to practice language in an engaging and encouraging way talking about images full of stories.

Dori Jacobsohn, the early childhood specialist who facilitated the discussion on *Child with a Dove*, also addresses why discussions are a particularly useful preschool tool:

> For language to develop in children, they must be engaged in conversations. It's not just a matter of hearing a lot of words, nor of being asked to recite words—naming things for example—but a matter of having meaningful exchanges using language—conversation, verbal give and take, negotiations. Children not only need to be introduced to language but also must become active players in communication. They need to hear how words are used, how they impact another. This is how they take in and compute meaning from words directed at them.[2]

If children must communicate orally to learn, we have another matter to consider: what do they talk about, what subjects or topics? An appropriate topic has two obvious requirements: first, the topic must interest children for them to engage. Second, children must feel they have something to say about it. As you already know, the topics of VTS discussions are carefully selected works of art.

ART TO JUMP-START THINKING AND LANGUAGE

Asking children to talk about images plays to strengths that all sighted children have—looking carefully and making sense of what they see. This section first dissects the reasons for this visual intelligence and then becomes more practical with ideas for how to find images to use in discussions. Sprinkled throughout the book are examples that have worked to stimulate many productive discussions with preschool children (see figure 2.1).[3]

FIGURE 2.1   Velino Shije Herrera, *Story Teller*

Theory: Addressing Developmental Issues

Children figure things out by looking from the time they open their eyes as infants. Tiny babies quickly recognize their parents, caregivers, and siblings and figure out that each attends to them in different ways. They soon realize that different expressions mean different things, a smile different from a worried look. We can see their awareness in their expressions. But this is just the beginning. Babies continue to search their worlds with their eyes, and as they grow, their visual insights build.

These visual insights are the basis for much early learning. Diane Zimmerman, a speech pathologist with an emphasis on child language development (and also a former elementary principal and school superintendent), sent the following thoughts on seeing and language in response to a variety of questions from me. She describes what she sees as the interplay between the two:

> The baby's understanding of the visual world explodes during the first months and years. They learn to look and point at what interests them. An entire industry of hard cardboard books has sprung up to aid parents in fostering looking and learning. During their second year, their babbling explodes into a cacophony of words and two-word utterances. The third year of life, however, is the real miracle. Somehow, without much prompting, the child begins to create sentences stringing many words together to follow syntax for the native language. The richer the language environment, the more vocabulary the child has with which to understand the world. The richer the visual environment, the more that vocabulary is anchored in the brain.[4]

Thoughtful caregivers know they are responsible for creating these language and visual environments. The richness of these environments varies from family to family and is complicated by demographics, socioeconomic status, and non-English-speaking parents and caregivers, for example, and these are not small matters. They are among the reasons preschool is essential: it gives a year or more to help minimize some of the differences in language preparedness of children and to ready all of them for later English language requirements.

Playing on a child's incessant looking, parents and caretakers who know to do so name what the baby's gaze seems to rest on. They chat with the child about what happens during the course of days—while eating, taking walks, playing, bathing, and so on. They narrate walks through parks, zoos, and stores, connecting what is seen and experienced to what is said.

Diane has a great story that describes two different parental styles contributing to a "word gap" that exists among children entering preschool. "This word gap is well researched and well documented," Diane wrote to me, "But what is not stated in this research is that the words a child knows for the most part have a visual referent. So not only have some children learned more words, but also they have looked at more things in their world." She goes on:

> Consider these two trips to the store. One mother encourages her son to hurry up, and when he complains and acts out, she puts him in the basket, pulls a toy out of her bag, then keeps on going. A mother of another young child puts him in a cart basket seat as well, but at each step of the way, she labels what she is buying, telling the child who in the family likes a particular food and responding when the baby points at food by naming it. Both of these parenting styles are positive for the child; the difference is that one is looking and learning, the other, simply playing with a well-worn toy, which he could do at home. One child is being comforted, but essentially ignored; the other is being enriched. When these parenting styles play out over and over, a vast difference in the spoken word exposure develops with impact on the level of vocabulary. It is as if these children live in two different worlds.[5]

It's likely that both mothers introduce the cardboard books Diane referred to, some early ones offering both visual and tactile opportunities, such as that famous bunny with a cotton tail there to pat. Books produced for babies as they become toddlers contain stories told in pictures more than words—for example, the much beloved *Goodnight Moon*.[6] It's almost impossible not to point to the objects mentioned in the text while looking at the book together.

Such illustrations do more than reflect the stories told in text, however. In many cases, they enrich the story greatly with detail and nuance skipped over in the simplicity of the text-told story. *Goodnight Moon* is a perfect example. More and more wordless books are available, too, usually with superb illustrations that tell a story through images alone. While at first, it's the adult who does that talking, asking the child to talk—even baby talk—about what she or he sees causes the tables to turn before long.

Research exists to help explain what's happening in a child's brain that results in the gap Diane referred to. One insight is that the child is exercising neural connections between what is seen, said, and heard, an important aspect of cognition: the child's "eye-mind connection," as I like to think of it. These connections—between perceptions, thinking, and language—have been studied many ways, including recently by neuroscientists trying to understand how the brain works. As presented most of the time, though, brain science is hard for us lay people to understand; an exception is Janneke van Leeuwen's *The Thinking Eye: Shaping Open Minds*, a booklet that makes understanding related brain processes clear, in part through illustrations, rare in the literature.[7] Van Leeuwen's work in neuroscience was partly inspired by VTS, and her condensation of research represents another rarity: making connections between scientific knowledge and how to apply that knowledge at home or in the classroom. Most scientists leave it to practitioners to figure out how to benefit from what's been learned.

Many years before the invention of tools that allow the scanning of brain activity, gestalt psychologist Rudolf Arnheim spent part of his long professional life minutely detailing evidence of the relationship between thinking and seeing. His research was empirical, meaning that he carefully observed human behavior over time (as did other much admired theoreticians, including Jean Piaget, Lev Vygotsky, and John Dewey). Arnheim eventually drew conclusions from those observations. He described what he'd seen and what he'd eventually concluded from it in his 1969 book *Visual Thinking*.[8]

Arnheim explored how the eyes collect perceptions that are passed along to different areas of the brain so swiftly that there is no point in separating the act of seeing from the process of thinking about what we see—the cognition involved in making sense of what is observed. The brain needs very little time to compute meaning from a visual encounter with a ball, a dog, or the possibility of danger because of associations between what we see and what we've come to know by way of earlier encounters.

This activity within the brain explains how, without instruction, infants begin to make connections between things—recognizing both an actual thing and a picture of it, for example. Over time they make additional connections: between things seen and the sounds of words attached to them, also because of neural interaction. In good time, what Diane refers to as the "miracle of language" begins to emerge from the child who gradually pieces together perceptions, thinking, and words.

Arnheim's book is dense, but over his long career as both scholar and teacher, he wrote much that makes it clear that educators can and should take seriously the visual capacities of children, and the relationship between seeing and language—the "eye-mind connection." It's no accident that VTS is called "Visual Thinking Strategies." Arnheim supplied the rationale for VTS discussions of images by preschoolers. And VTS is named in honor of him.

With Arnheim as an inspiration, VTS cocreator Abigail Housen showed in her Harvard doctoral thesis that earliest meaning making expressed with words might be referred to as taking a visual inventory—looking and then naming what you see.[9] You saw evidence of that basic process in the first two discussion samples about *Child with a Dove* and *Domino Players*. It's not an orderly inventory or a complete one, but it includes what stands out to the viewers, what they recognize from experience. Housen would argue that what isn't known already might not even be noticed until someone else points it out and names it. She has also found that idiosyncratic observation—common among preschoolers—is a natural developmental phenomenon; even adults new to art will make observations that make sense to them but are harder for others to see.

Practice: Thinking About Images for Your Students

In VTS, we play to the human interest in making observations by showing groups of children objects depicting familiar and recognizable people, places, things, and activities, like the family grouping in figure 2.2.[10] What one child doesn't recognize might be identified by another or seen as something different entirely. Some of what there is to see will simply be bypassed. In any case, to fire up the discussions, we search for images that children enjoy and contain enough that is familiar to prompt many observations. Knowing your students as you do should guide you to find images you want to use—what they will recognize and be able to talk about.

Soon the accumulation of observations becomes the basis for an additional kind of thinking. We call this inferring or, said differently using Housen's language, rudimentary storytelling, which is something we saw with Erika's kids: "She's stirring her porridge," for example.

To encourage the behaviors of inferring or finding stories, the meanings of images used for discussions must be accessible. For example, a picture with people sitting around a table makes it a modest stretch for kids to infer they might be eating or playing a game. Or thinking about the picture in figure 2.1—one that might naturally encourage counting as well as story finding—"I think the man is telling a story."

Finding images with uncomplicated, recognizable narratives is easy; humans have used art to tell stories since the beginning of time. All you need to do is think about what stories your particular class of kids will find most interesting to consider.

FIGURE 2.2   Maria Izquierdo, *My Nieces (Mis Sobrinas)*

We steer away from images that are dense, murky, macabre, or scary. It's not that children cannot deal with these images in some ways, but we prefer to give them images that allow them to compute meanings that add to their trove of memories in positive ways. There is enough time later for the broader range of options our very visual world produces.

We also avoid abstract imagery often thought to be a natural for kids because of how their own drawings, especially early ones, resemble abstractions. In truth, the resemblance is superficial. Children aren't thinking or drawing abstractly; their brains are not yet wired for the formal and reductive thinking that motivates artists of abstractions. In my view, drawing is a natural means for children to express thoughts while different vocabularies are in the process of developing. Over time, their drawings naturally turn to representation of what they see in the world just as they go from baby talk to using words we understand to say what they want or mean.

When asked to discuss abstract pictures, young ones will name what they see, but using such pictures is actually a setup for eccentric observations, a natural phenomenon but something children will outgrow if they are encouraged to probe the meanings of activities in the world we share—the so-called real world. In other words, we prefer to see imagination put to work in the service of examining perceptions deeply and creatively, using their natural inventiveness to probe expressions, interactions, implied emotions, for example. What they find in abstract art is not interesting to them in the way that mining for meanings told by more naturally representative characters and settings is—and finding meaning is more valuable developmentally than naming things that aren't really there.

Nudes are illogical choices too in order to respect the values of children's home environments, which are very diverse in the contemporary world. Again, it's not that children cannot deal with these images at some level, but that impressionable young minds and the complications of our melting pot nation suggest the wisdom of our letting such subjects be handled at home.

Another factor comes into play in choosing images for discussion. While appropriate artworks must depict many elements children recognize quickly, they must contain others that are up for debate—ones that provoke a range of opinions. The images that stimulated our samples and others in this book all have the combination. For example, a figure could be a boy or a girl, shapes could be one thing or another. The people in the circle might be listening to the man. Ladies standing around a table could be eating or making food, as in figure 2.3.[11]

Some Details

Study the images included with the lessons cited here and elsewhere in this book to help you choose ones that might work for the children in your life. Also, keep in mind that what is familiar to children who have lived only in cities and those for whom rural sites are the norm may be slightly different. The point is to find images to engage the young ones

FIGURE 2.3   Fred Beaver (*Eka La Nee [Brown Head]*), *Florida Seminoles Preparing Food*

quickly and also keep them interested for a while using what they know collectively to figure out what they are looking at.

Even with all these provisos, it's not hard to find such art. People have made images for millennia. One of the defining characteristics of art is its remarkable combination of what is familiar and what is puzzling, like the shoes and hair in the image of the child with the dove in figure 1.1. Some illustrations in books qualify too, though others are too simple to be good topics for conversation.

The Internet and computers make it easier to find and use images than ever before, and the array to choose from is staggering. To get a sense of this, go to Google Images and search for "children playing together in art works" or "families in art."[12] A huge number of pictures like figure 2.2 will come up quickly, ranging from silly to serious, diverse in time and story, and somewhat diverse in terms of demographics and ethnicities. You can also search for images or artists you know. You can search for versions of any of the images in this book by using the artist and title of the work. You'll likely find more than one example of the picture. Choose the biggest; it's likely to be the best. You'll also see others displayed that might appeal to you for your students.

Once you've found pictures you want to try, find a way to capture and project them; ask your school's media person or your favorite techie to find out how if you don't already know. I find putting a series of pictures in a PowerPoint slide presentation useful, thinking ahead and choosing many possibilities as long as I'm searching, but the point is to find the best way to show images large enough for all to see. If you use PowerPoint, you can make notes within the presentation if you want to recall what students said and/or your overall opinion about the usefulness of a picture—data for future reference.

Once in the classroom, show the picture on a screen or board low enough so that children can directly point to something if they need to show you what they see. A flat-screen television, Smart Boards, and other interactive tools will also work as long as you can connect it to a computer.

In Summary

The use of art in VTS is based on its effectiveness as a resource that stimulates observing, thinking out loud, and storytelling; you also use it because it provides a special kind of imagery that you want to include in the visual treasure chest of children of all backgrounds when they are still young. Art tends to live beyond its time often because generation after generation of people perceive it to be about something important. We want to make sure children's exposure to images includes art and begins early, something that is not guaranteed as modern life unfolds for most people. As explained by Lise White of the Charlestown Nursery School: "The fact that VTS uses fine art is important. It's very respectful of young children to let them look at fine art and to recognize they have a connection to it. It shows how capable young children are: they are fully able to connect to and deal with the complexity of art."[13]

Lev Vygotsky, a Russian student of early childhood behavior, documented many young children talking their way through tasks as they figured out what they were supposed to do. As soon as language is available to them, he pointed out, children begin talking themselves into learning what they come to know. The task in the VTS case is meaning making. With VTS, we give children the chance to engage their eye-mind connection, use their growing language ability to probe the visual complexities (and to do so with assists from peers), and in effect use art to help them learn to think. We help them down the road toward visual literacy too.

All that to convey why discussion and why art are key elements in VTS and important in early childhood teaching! Now it's time to move onto the next element: the moment of silence asked for as soon as the image is shown to children.

MOMENTS OF SILENCE

I like the way that the time to look in silence is described by colleague Kay Cutler: "If we give children time to guide themselves into the stories told by examining the images, they use their remarkable ability to look, figure out the meaning of what they see, and turn that into communication."[14] Kay is a professor of education at South Dakota State University (Brookings) and director of the Fishback Center for Childhood Education there. She's been watching VTS in use for five years and is convinced that silent looking is one of the most important aspects of VTS.

Children, like most of us, live fast-paced lives these days with many activities and options available most of the time and also many potential distractions. Animated programs and computer games are high on that list. For children to immerse themselves in a slow-moving, focused, reflective activity such as VTS, we need to give them arresting pictures—and a moment to stop, look, and think before jumping into action.

It's best not to predetermine an arbitrary amount of time but tell the children that you want them to take a few moments just to look. Sarah O'Leary turns the silent looking into a well-defined task: "I want you to look carefully at this picture. Go from top to bottom and from the left side to the right. See how much you can notice." Of course, she points in the relevant directions as she gives the instructions both to underscore the assignment and to help children remember which side is right and which is left.

You can also try something like Sarah does to keep them at their task: "I love that you are still looking and showing focus." If you regularly undertake other activities intended to slow things down—like yoga, meditation, or mindfulness—link this activity to those. Help the children understand that taking time is purposeful.

Meanwhile, look at the picture yourself to model the behavior as well as keeping your eyes open for signs of jumpiness, an indication that it's time to ask the opening question. The period of looking might get longer as children become more accustomed to the task. See what they can handle.

Teacher Erin Jeanneret mentions this opening period of silence as being a rare and significant part of what VTS introduces. She puts it this way: "It's great to take time. It even helps me slow down. It's useful to remember that taking time leads to finding more."[15] Although I think Erin would not make this distinction, my thought is that this slowing down might be particularly helpful for children living intensely urban lives, like the ones she teaches. Seven years ago, Erin joined the faculty of Mott Haven Academy, a new charter school in the South Bronx, a mostly black and Hispanic neighborhood in New York City—more than half the population are Spanish speaking and most are low income. Erin isn't likely to mention any of this information; she sees her class of eighteen children as she would any group: young capable people who are ready and able to learn.

In my view, the very urban experience and extraordinary stress of city kids' lives makes a quiet moment of looking especially helpful. Erin sees it as "an aspect of VTS that carries over to other parts of the day. The quiet looking makes an impact on what is noticed in general."[16] Her class is roughly divided by thirds—one-third of the children from the neighborhood; one-third in foster care (though perhaps with a family member); and one-third in the care of the child welfare system because of homelessness, an incarcerated parent, or a caregiver with drug abuse issues. Erin says that the differences among the students in each third are rarely clear, but some come with greater language preparation, which is useful because of the way students scaffold on each other's abilities during discussions.

Nora Elton has taught preschool classes in a range of schools spanning the spectrum of neighborhoods.[17] Her comments on working with classes in two public schools in East Boston, an area similar to the South Bronx in terms of demographics, note some differences worth mentioning while addressing the element of silent looking. One of the schools had once been a Montessori school, and Nora saw influences of the method still in play, one of them being a kind of calm and deliberateness that seemed to pervade the classroom.

Another preschool where Nora worked was part of a more typical public school, and she heard reports from teachers in other grades that they were surprised at the ability of the preschool kids to focus as they do during silent looking and during VTS discussions in general. In her view, if silent looking "did nothing but prove that children are capable of focus," she was delighted. "It's important for children to get a lesson in looking in preschool. It's also good that they are seen as capable of focus by their teachers."[18] Expectations often set low bars for performance, so seeing children as capable of focus can contribute to positive assumptions about their potential. Few of us admit to thinking of children as limited in terms of capabilities, but surprise at the ability of little ones to focus points to the existence of such views.

Since we've reflected on the reflective moment of silence, it's time to move on to how we put an end to the reverie and put the conversation into motion. In VTS, we initiate this conversation with well-studied questions.

THE QUESTIONS

The Opening Questions

Two pedagogical principles motivate the use of questions in teaching. One is the age-old adage that we learn most from doing—and the doing in this case is looking, thinking, and talking. The other principle is that activity benefits from some direction if it is to result in learning. Children are gifted at following their noses; the right question will help them direct their attention for a worthwhile purpose.

That said, what makes a good question if you want to activate and direct three- or four-year-olds?

For one thing, the meaning of the question has to be clear. The behavior or answer you are looking for must be apparent immediately. In addition, the instruction should be open-ended, with no specific answer wanted, so that children can answer in their own ways. Furthermore, the directive must be something children find compelling.

For the most part, we omit questions that seek right or wrong answers or specific information. Most preschoolers will try to answer such questions, for sure, but some will be left scratching their heads. If they do try to answer and if their responses are off base or fanciful, what benefit is that to any of them? What do they learn if they are wrong, except for the dreadful lesson that they failed at something? This view reflects my attitude toward the academic learning that is being requested and even required of many public preschools.

You already know that I was skeptical whether questions that worked for third or fifth or even first graders would work for younger children, but only minor tweaking was, in fact, required. Lise White, who teaches the youngest children at the Charlestown Nursery School, offered this reflection on the preferred phrasing of the opening question that has worked for her with children at the younger ages of the preschool spectrum. In response to a question from me, she offered, "When doing a VTS lesson with toddlers, particularly in the beginning of the year, we often ask, 'What do you see?' and 'What do you notice?' as well as 'What's going on in this picture?'"[19] This last question can be used with older students in preschool as it is in the elementary grades.

I heard the first two phrasings frequently while visiting preschool classes doing research for this book. "What do you see?" I had thought some years before, would be useful with very young children because of its clear meaning. Kids do a lot of looking; they know how to see. I learned from site visits that "What do you notice?" is a similarly familiar request to children, and it therefore helps them open discussions, particularly when VTS is new to them. I've heard this phrase also thrown in from time to time during discussions, particularly when you know a child wants to speak but is tongue-tied when actually given the chance. "What do you notice?" seems to empower them.

In reflecting on these two verbs—see and notice—and the instruction built in to both, it seems to me that notice encompasses more than see. Seeing asks for a basic perceptual behavior, finding what is obvious to the child. Noticing incorporates seeing but also implies "What do you recognize?" Or "What do you know from life that you find in this picture?" This distinction might seem like splitting hairs, but children at these responsive ages tend to be literal; they will try to do what is asked. Asking them to comment on what they notice opens the door to meaning making, whereas asking for what they see focuses on observations alone.

Observing is the most basic behavior, as Housen tells us; meaning making based on observations is within reach, however. It is within what Vygotsky labeled the "zone of proximal development": those behaviors of which one is capable with perhaps a slight nudge (as in the right question) or a gentle assist (as provided by peers whose development is a bit ahead).

The opening question used with older students works in the later ages of preschool, three and four: *"What's going on in this picture?"* or *"What's happening in this picture?"* The nature of the wording enables children simply to share observations if that is what they want to do. You observed that response in the discussions of both *Child with a Dove* (figure 1.1) and *Domino Players* (figure 1.2). But the wording also gives permission for students to respond another way: finding meanings based on observations, or, said differently, identifying stories they find. The children in Erika's class responded with stories from the start while examining *Le Gourmet* (figure 1.3).

Research has shown us why children identify stories. Making observations—the task inherent in "What do you see?" particularly—is the most basic looking behavior. If that was ever in question, we saw ample evidence of this in the discussion Dori led ("There's a boy.") and some of it in Sarah's discussion as well—for example, "I see the red thing" or "I see a crown." We saw an even earlier form of observing from the child Marta, who either didn't know the word or, more likely, was too shy to say "ball." She therefore got up and pointed. Dori then supplied the word. All of these examples are typical and appropriate behaviors from which children grow as their VTS discussions (which might be called "structured looking") continue to build experience.

Nothing that a child says is wrong with any of the questions, of course. In all cases, you are asking what the children find in the image—not what you see, but what they find there. It's their call to answer in the ways that occur to them.

It can take as few as ten or twelve discussions for the "What's going on . . ." formulation of the question to begin to take hold with all students and for simple observing to give way to the significantly more complex behavior: students beginning to infer things from what is observed. Here's an early form of inferring: "I see that they have some white things on." It's not just "I see white"; it seems as if the child understands that the white in *Domino Players* implies some sort of garment people are wearing. Or in an ever so slightly less advanced version of inferring, "They are eating." While the latter is a simple sentence, representative of slowly developing verbal skills, the child's thinking has advanced from observation to inference.

Here's an example of inferred meaning slightly further along, taken from the discussion led by Erika: "It looks like she doesn't have a mom or dad." When Lara made this comment during the discussion of *Le Gourmet*, she continued a discussion of the figure in the picture, but having noticed that the child is alone, she inferred that the child had no parents. It's as if Lara was telling a story.

Another sample inference, really a pair of inferences in the discussion about *Le Gourmet*—"*There's a little girl standing up* and *eating her porridge*"—is expressed in more complex and detailed language too. To some extent, the language is driven by the compound nature of the thought, but it's also because of Ana's language environment, a combination of what's happening in the preschool building and at home.

The development we've tracked from simple observations to detailed inferences doesn't happen by accident. The framing of the question helps drive this change, as do comments from "more capable peers," Vygotsky's phrase. Other factors influencing such change include time itself (children grow and change so quickly), as well as more talking, more listening, more exposure to books, and very likely instruction itself. VTS is a part of this: all these factors compound to produce that kind of change in thought and language.

I put instruction last here because, knowing the school this child attends, I know the teachers do a lot of informal teaching but not a lot of direct instruction of the sort that many public preschools are required to do. I will add again my view of such priorities: preschools conform not necessarily because children are ready or because the instruction actually sticks as learning—as teachers know—but because the system demands they do so.

The Second Question

To help build from the predictable idiosyncrasy of beginning viewers of any age, the formulation of VTS for grades starting with kindergarten includes a second question, one that has been seen as useful in many contexts. This question asks for evidence: *"What do you see that makes you say that?"*

Applying this question in preschool requires a judgment call on the part of the teacher. You need to decide when in the year and with whom it's a fair question, one that a child is developmentally ready to answer. Talking about what children notice and what is going on in pictures is a task virtually all handle easily. Providing evidence is a more challenging category of task. Of course, it's not about seeking a right answer from children—just details from the picture rooted in their perceptions—but still it asks for evidential reasoning, a so-called higher-level thinking skill.

Because of the developmental issue, I was particularly skeptical about whether this question was appropriate to include in preschool VTS at all when my colleague Paula Lynn first made moves to try VTS with very young children. She also wondered about the wisdom of including this question, but as with much she did, she thought about the question's function in a broader context than simply to build the habit of providing evidence. She recently sent me this useful reflection on the matter, one that also introduces another possible question that can be used to achieve an additional objective she clearly articulates: stimulating more language.

> At the start of the year I struggled a bit with the VTS questions as they were written for grades K–2. The preschool students were most often offering one-word comments with very little description. My instinct was that I wanted them to use more words during each turn and build their description skills. It seemed to me that being able to describe something was a necessary skill to build so that eventually, when developmentally appropriate, they would be able to provide the visual evidence to support their ideas.
>
> When I tried asking, "What do you see that makes you say that?" I thought that they would likely provide circular reasoning but at least they would be using more words to express themselves. And the question did help a few students describe in more detail but it, unfortunately, confounded the majority of the students. I took this issue to Abigail Housen [coauthor of VTS] who often helped me reflect on my work and we talked through a few different approaches. In the end, given that my goal was to encourage the use of language, communication, and description, I might follow up responses with something like, "Tell me more about that." And it worked. After a few lessons I began using the "tell me more about that" prompt often and found that in addition to encouraging description, it also oriented them to the VTS discussion structure of a probing question following their initial comment.[20]

As I have observed teachers using VTS, in part as research for this book, I've heard them ask if students could "tell me more about that." I have traditionally viewed use of the question through the lens of VTS in elementary schools where it's not a good question; students usually say what they have to say in their response to "What's going on?" and provide additional detail adequately when asked for evidence. In preschool, I think that, like the use of "What do you notice?" it can encourage children to add to their simple opening comments. It serves the purpose that Paula articulates. I think it might be best applied to children who are inclined to speak very little and might need added encouragement. If in your judgment a child has commented "at capacity," I wouldn't press for more; a child with whom it's definitely inappropriate is one who gets up to point to what she or he has noticed.

Another context where I'd use this approach sparingly is a class of fifteen or more students, as so many preschools have. You can't dwell too long with many students; otherwise, you shortchange others. Or you protract the discussion until students get antsy. Bottom line: it's useful to remember that you can ask "Could you tell me more?" when it appears to you that a fruitful answer will be forthcoming, one that benefits the child and the group because of its inherent inspiration for language use.

Preschool-age children won't recognize what's going on for them cognitively, but many soon know what to do when the teacher poses the second question. A few might actually start applying it on their own, particularly if this question finds its way into teachers' methods more generally. Sarah O'Leary recently commented, "We used VTS today to explore our incubator as we prepare to hatch ducks. 'What did you see/hear/notice that made you say that?' is a natural part of our conversations regardless of the context."[21] If children are habitually asked to supply evidence, it becomes a habit to do so. Our intention is to help children develop this useful habit beginning very young.

Remember that the meaning of this question might not be immediately clear, and to many, it's not a fair task when starting this process. Phase in the question based on who's ready, particularly considering those at the younger ages in nursery school. That said, you've seen by way of the previous sample discussions that answering this question is within reach of most students given a little experience. The combination of coming to understand what the question asks, of hearing the teacher's supportive responses, and of following the example of other children—peer learning, that immensely powerful tool—helps nurture the behavior in those younger or simply slower to take to the task.

The Third Question

The third VTS question is *"What more can we find?"* and it's used from the start of discussion. Like the first two questions, the phrasing evolved over time as we watched responses to different ways of seeking a particular behavior. In this case, the behavior sought was for viewers to develop the habit of looking beyond what they first notice. To do so often produces more detail, and that, in turn, provides food for richer inferences.

Use the question between each comment, as you call on a new student. What we've seen is that continually inserting this third question, even when lots of hands are raised, lets children know there's always more to find if they keep looking. This is one of the great aspects of using art as the focus of conversations. It easily yields more information upon longer looking and reflection.

As important, since ideas emerge one at a time, "What more can we find?" prolongs the discussion, thus allowing for earlier comments, not just the image itself, to become food for thought. Disagreements are the easiest way to see this: "No, it IS a girl!" Bella emphatically responded to Dori. But look back to the discussion of *Le Gourmet* to see what followed the comment Lara introduced: "It looks like she doesn't have a mom or dad." Her comment provoked a chain of responses, most of them building on the unfolding story of missing parents. In addition to the insertion of other sorts of comments, children continued to add new possibilities to the missing parent story, the one they found particularly worth pursuing. We think that hearing the third question again and again assists in developing a habit of this kind of probing, a skill that is useful in language literacy later.

Summary of the Questions

These three questions taken together provoke a pattern of looking and thinking. I emphasize pattern because the three build on one another and cohere usefully. Once the pattern is internalized—and it doesn't take all that long—it becomes a meaning-making system and can be applied any time a child encounters something only partially familiar or something worth examining (such as watching duck eggs about to hatch). And you can hear the questions in use around preschool classrooms. They apparently stick with teachers and students.

Dori Jacobsohn told me one particularly wonderful example: "Recently, I observed a five-year-old organize a group of kids and 'pretend' teach with a wordless picture book. She said, 'What's happening on this page?' She pointed and repeated what the children said. The kids were captivated." Dori further explained: "She'd had two VTS discussions before she did this. These were kids from highly educated upper middle class families with many experiences and big vocabularies, but even then it amazed and delighted me."[22]

This teacher-in-the-making had internalized the process after two lessons. This child may have come from a privileged background, but so do kids in many preschools. The insight that I take away from this instance is that at some level, the questions and process made sense to her. That the other children played along suggests VTS resonated with them as well.

This happens with all children, not just the privileged. One of the reasons this is so and that the VTS questions are memorable is that, while they structure the looking process, they do so by means that invoke natural and instinctive responses to images and other sorts of phenomena children see. Also, the questions are used at the moments when they are helpful. Children experience the questions extending something they enjoy and in which they are deeply engaged. No one asks children to remember the questions, but they do. Not always word for word, but they stick.

The questions used in VTS come from many years of research. The original opening question—"What's going on/happening in this picture?"—was formulated based on data already collected by cognitive scholar Abigail Housen over the many years she studied how viewers behaved when looking at art. The other two questions of the set—"What do you see that makes you say that?" and "What more can we find?"—built on both existing data of Housen's and data collected as together we went through the iterative process of studying the results. If the questions we used weren't stimulating the responses wanted, we tweaked them, which usually involved a matter of simplifying.

Bottom line: we saw that together the questions create a pattern of looking and thinking that enables examining and constructing meaning from diverse images—and even incubators with duck eggs. As a result, the questions stick well enough that both teachers and children naturally use them over and over.

LISTENING, POINTING, AND PARAPHRASING

I lump the next three elements together because they are three pieces of a process that create a meaningful whole: to know what children say, you have to listen carefully. Pointing shows you're following along, and you see what they are talking about. Paraphrasing proves you've not only heard their words but understand what they mean. Each of these elements came into being as thoughtfully as the questions evolved.

Listening

Listening as carefully and thoughtfully as VTS asks is often described as "active listening"—defined by Wikipedia as "requiring that the listener fully concentrate, understand, respond and then remember what is being said."[23]Active listening is most often used in problem resolution and different sorts of counseling where misunderstandings might be a partial cause of conflict. Active listening in these situations is usually coupled with repeating what you've heard to prove that you got it.

In the case of VTS, listening is part of nurturing learners, not resolving conflicts. It's aligned with active listening because of what it requires—concentration, understanding, responding, and remembering. A VTS teacher does all these in part for practical reasons: you can neither point nor paraphrase if you haven't heard what a child is talking about. The importance of hearing kids goes way beyond VTS. Listening to children is an essential aspect of nurturing them.

Rudolf Arnheim, the scholar who coined the phrase "visual thinking," made a wonderful statement that reads "the best teacher is not the one who deals out all he knows or who withholds all he could give, but the one who, with the wisdom of a good gardener, watches, judges, and helps out when help is needed."[24]

This thinking makes sense to me. Who doesn't benefit from help when needed, from comfort and caring? On the other hand, few of us grow in an environment of constant challenge. As schools have become driven by goals of academic achievement—measured by tests—the notion of the teacher as helper, guide, and nurturer has diminished. VTS is something teachers can use to dissipate any sense of pressure and engage children in a slower, essentially nurturing activity. I see willingness to listen as a key aspect of "the wisdom of a good teacher." It's an acknowledgment of respect for young learners.

Listening attentively, which most of us think we do, is put to the test in VTS. It's more work than we expect even to concentrate in the focused manner required; we don't do it as often as we think, in part because of expectations: we know what we want to hear and also think we know what someone is going to say.

Listening to preschool-age people is particularly challenging. Ideas we didn't imagine come up often and make it hard to grasp quickly what is meant. Understanding the language choices and articulation make it difficult. Shy, small voices are hard to hear. Comments are often very brief and seem to leave out a lot. We sometimes have to push for clarifications and even ask children to come show us what they are talking about.

Nevertheless, listening is worth the effort. Sensing someone listens and hears what you say can seem like a gift. And if it happens too rarely—as is often the case—one can end up feeling isolated and/or incompetent. It's never okay to feel that way, but particularly as children enter the great adventure called school. If listening and proving we are doing so can help children feel valued, it's worth making listening a constant practice. Besides, who can learn to listen if they have no models to show what it is and what comes of it?

Pointing

Pointing is the next part of the trio of elements that nest comfortably together. This element sounds easy enough, but to make sure you're prepared, study the picture you're intending to use. Knowing the image makes finding what interests the children much easier. And it makes it much more likely you'll be able to fathom what they see when they are unclear or idiosyncratic.

Using your pointer finger usually works. Point to what is mentioned with precision. Outline the silhouette of a figure, for example, or when a child is talking about, say, a group of people at a table, closely encircle the area with your finger.

Point as a child speaks. Your intention is to show that you see what she or he does; it's a visual paraphrase. Meanwhile, you help keep everyone's eyes focused on the picture. In the case of less obvious observations and small details, you direct everyone's eyes to the relevant place, object, person, or activity, perhaps calling attention to a part of the picture others may have missed.

During the discussion, what comes to the attention of children is unpredictable and some of it quirky. If you can't find what is meant as you scan the image, ask for clarification: "Do you mean this?" Or say "I think I need help finding that." If, after a further comment, you still can't find it, ask the child to come show you (and everyone else) what she or he has found. Since some children become tongue-tied when it's their turn to speak, it's smart to ask them first to use their words but good naturedly let them approach the picture if they can't. You never want children to feel inadequate during VTS, so give them room to be who they are, including reticent.

Pointing serves another purpose: it helps you remember what's been mentioned. And you need to recall all that's said so you can paraphrase the comments, the next element to address here.

Paraphrasing

Paraphrasing is your way of doing several things. The first is most immediately important: you show children that you hear and value what they say; their comments matter. Since little growth results from sitting back, you want all children to participate; therefore, making sure they know that anything they say will be okay is essential. That "anything you say is okay" thing is what's missing with a lot of other questions, and it's why VTS questions were thought through so carefully. Though the questions imply open-endedness, your response to comments confirms that you truly want to know what they think and that's all you care about. The purpose of the discussion is not about you, or even the picture, really; it's about what they find.

Lise White, who teaches toddlers (two- and three-year-olds) at the Charlestown Nursery School, describes paraphrasing and its intentions beautifully:

> Paraphrasing ensures that the teacher facilitating the VTS lesson is listening to the child who is speaking. It also amplifies the voice of the child speaking and tunes in the ears of the children listening. Paraphrasing validates the ideas and observations of the children, sending the message, "I am listening closely to what you are saying, and offering your message back to you and your peers. What you are saying is worth hearing."[25]

Quickly on the heels of that in order of importance to children's growth is the assistance paraphrasing gives them with language itself. As you've seen, preschoolers' responses to images range from having something to say but not being able to spit it out to very short sentences that leave much to the listener's imagination to fairly explicit, reasonably articulated thoughts. Pointing ensures you have heard what they say; paraphrasing ensures you've understood it. It's not always easy to find other words for simple thoughts, but you can almost invariably put the comment into a sentence. Here's an example from the discussion of *Child with a Dove*; notice what Dori did:

> DORI: *What's happening in this picture?*
> ADAM: *There's a boy.*
> DORI: *You're noticing this figure in the center, and you're thinking it might be boy. What do you see that makes you say it's a boy?*
> ADAM: *Boys have hair like that.*
> DORI: *So you're noticing the hairstyle and it reminds you of the way a boy might wear his hair. What more can we find?*

What Dori did here was not just about finding other words, but also demonstrating the bigger picture of communication. She didn't change what Adam said, and she stayed true to what he meant. Yet she first described what he had done—"noticed the figure in the center"—and how he identified what he saw—"There's a boy." In response to Adam's answer to the second question, she mentioned what he pointed to as evidence—"Boys have hair like that."—as well as what cognition had taken place to lead him to that conclusion. She said, "It reminds you . . ." of what you know: "the way a boy might wear his hair."

Note that she repeatedly used the word *might* when she paraphrased the conclusion Adam drew—"it *might* be a boy," "the way a boy *might* wear his hair." We refer to this as using conditional language—words that convey that something is possible if that's what you see—but still allows room for other interpretations. You likely recall that Bella did see that boy differently and didn't like Dori's "might be a girl" phrasing of her thought. Yes, it was irritating to Bella, but even as an apparently very confident four-year-old, she stopped insisting. And that's the point. Qualifying her comment makes more openings for later speakers, keeps the discussion going, and is early training in the fact that relatively few things in this world are exactly as they appear.

Only a few minutes later, Jon pointed out that some girls have short hair too. Jon might not have added this comment if Dori had paraphrased Adam by saying, "It's a boy because boys have short hair." My guess is that Bella was a strong enough character to have asserted another conclusion about the figure, but I wonder if Jon might not have just let the matter drop.

This is the kind of thing we thought about for the many years we worked on refining VTS. What we sought were the essential elements that would elicit a range of thoughts and therefore provoke good conversations, ones worth listening to. What we wanted was that kids would listen as hard as teachers do, equally intent on understanding what's said and responding to it when they wished.

Listening and paraphrasing are the kinds of tasks that makes VTS harder to do than it looks. The teacher must keep a whole lot in mind, and the tasks conflict to some degree. You have to be 100 percent present to hear what children say. At virtually the same time, you also have to be in your head enough to think about what they mean, how you can rephrase their responses productively and supportively, and how to put your paraphrase into conditional language. Ideally, you'll mention what kind of mental activity was involved on the part of the child—as in the hair "reminds" Adam of boys' hairstyles. We call that "framing" their thoughts, categorizing them.

I haven't listed framing as an element of VTS because although it is an aspect of VTS that's important in the long run and always helpful to the children, it's something you can wait to add to your facilitation until you're feeling very confident that you have all the questions internalized, and pointing, listening, and paraphrasing feel second nature. And they will.

When you do begin to frame, however, you'll be addressing a long-term benefit of VTS facilitation. One of today's more useful standards to be met over the course of elementary school is to want children to learn to think and at the very least be able to explain how they solve problems. By framing their thoughts now, you can help children start to understand thinking, even if that understanding remains subliminal for years. At preschool ages, children cannot be expected to recognize the ways VTS structures their experience in any direct or concrete sense. It's clearly germane for you to understand that this technique can be seminal, however.

LINKING

You already have a lot to keep in mind, of course, but I hope you can practice one more element as you learn VTS. We call it "linking." This example is near the end of the discussion Dori led on *Child with a Dove*. After yet another thought on the figure's gender, Pieter's comment, Dori said: "We have a different clue from the clothes. Bella thinks it's a girl because of the dress, and you noticed the style of shoes and speculate it might be a boy. We have a few different ideas about who this child might be." She acknowledged the discrepancies in interpretations just as she earlier said that, "Bella has another idea about the child . . ." Dori linked various ideas, some building on one another, others divergent.

Linking continuously during the discussion eliminates the need for a summary at the end but more importantly legitimizes different opinions. It's never too soon to learn that different views exist, and it's okay. "I can think this and you can think that," no problem. We learn that when we share views, discussions are richer for different ideas— and, not so by the way, so is our experience of this complicated, global society in which we live.

You will be forgiven if you think that so many elements make VTS a bit harder to do than it looks. One bit of advice that I've heard again and again from teachers beginning their VTS voyages is that memorizing the questions leaves you free to concentrate on your communication with each child. You can remain more present, less worried about what you might do next. As you can see, our sample teachers managed to learn it. While they are wonderful teachers, they aren't super human. They practiced VTS to get to where they are now. They took time, and it might take you a bit of time as well. If you are challenged at first, the process will get easier; if you make a mistake, you may be sure the kids will forgive you. They are delighted just to see that you listen.

SOME LAST THOUGHTS

Here are two final reflections for this analysis. The first is that teaching children to listen is difficult. You can ask children to do it, but that doesn't mean they will. And it's very difficult to know it's happening or to assess how the skill changes. My guess is that the way to teach listening is to demonstrate it: "I'm listening to you, and this is how I prove that." I think an important corollary is to routinely give children something worth listening to.

Similarly, I don't think it's possible to teach children to be self-confident. You can, however, set up circumstances that encourage willing participation, make sure that children feel comfortable being a part of a group or process, and find authentic ways to acknowledge and reward their personal risk taking.

In its structure, VTS seems to help in these two aspects of social and emotional development. We've consistently heard from preschool teachers that children do learn to listen to one another during VTS discussions and that their confidence grows over time, all the more so with children who seem to lack it at the start.

So here's the short of it: each element of VTS is part of a structure that intends to lead to growth—in observational skills; in oral expression; in thinking; in social skills such as listening, getting used to different opinions, and finding their own voice and the confidence to use it. It also provides a useful method for teachers to use in many circumstances.

AT A GLANCE: VTS FOR PRESCHOOL

Present a carefully selected image. Productive choices contain

- subjects of interest to very young children—children playing, parents and children interacting in familiar ways, animals doing something, and so on
- familiar imagery given the existing knowledge of students, therefore taking into account their varied life experiences
- simple storylines, narratives with accessible meaning, again thinking about the specific group of children you are teaching
- some ambiguity, or some room for interpretation

Allow a few moments of silent looking before beginning the discussion. Make it a task with specific directions: for example, look from top to bottom, then side to side; look for big details and small ones.

Pose specific research-tested questions to motivate and maintain the inquiry:

- Start with: What do you see in this picture? Or what do you notice?
- As soon as you think they are ready, change to: What's going on (or what's happening) in this picture? Ask this only at the beginning to get the discussion started.
- Also, when you think a child is ready and has said something open to interpretation, ask: What do you see that makes you say that?
- After each comment, ask: What more can you find?

Facilitate the discussion by

- listening carefully to catch all that students say; if they have no words, letting them come to the image and point. If you can't find what they see, asking for their help: can you show us what you're seeing? If you don't understand what they mean, also asking for help: can you add more words to help us understand?

- pointing to observations—a "visual paraphrase"—as students comment, and point again as you rephrase the idea
- paraphrasing each comment no matter how short, taking a moment to reflect if you need to; show you understand the child's meaning when you respond
- linking related comments whether students agree or disagree, or build on one another's ideas
- remaining neutral by treating everyone and each comment in the same way

Conclude by thanking students for their participation. Tell them what you particularly enjoyed. Suggest they share other ideas with someone sitting next to them.

CHAPTER 3

Adapting VTS
for Other Lessons

CARLY REAGAN AT THE Charlestown Nursery School has been including VTS in the classes she coteaches for three- and four-year-olds attending this remarkable private preschool for the past three years. I asked her for some reflections on those years. She responded:

> *Why do I continue to use VTS? I find it's great for the kids. One time when it can be particularly helpful is in the beginning of the year when everyone is getting to know others. Another moment is when I notice that a child has a hard time hearing others. VTS will come to the rescue! I think discussions build the sense that it's part of our job as people to listen and incorporate the ideas of others. These are the building blocks of some very large skills that kids need to know to meet the future—skills like being able to handle big ideas, to habitually offer evidence, to realize the value of the ideas of others even if contrary.[1]*

Carly is not alone in thinking that VTS serves many purposes. Virtually as soon as we started doing field research in schools—to make sure it produced the viewing skills we sought—we started getting reports from teachers who saw behaviors they appreciated but we never expected.

VTS was originally created to teach museum visitors skills they felt they needed to get more pleasure and meaning out of art. Because of its effectiveness at doing that, VTS is now taught in many museums here and abroad. Now twenty-five years later, we continue to learn why teachers value VTS, and Carly's commentary here is a wonderful case in point.

This chapter focuses on specific uses teachers have found for VTS once students were used to the practice with images. Beyond the reasons and advantages of using art to start with, in preschool we also have come to expect teachers to quickly try the strategy in other lessons, allowing for productive talk throughout their days.

VTS AND BOOKS

Probably the most frequent application of VTS in other preschool activities is while reading together. Once teachers have seen this strategy work with art images, they rarely resist the chance to apply it to art's next of kin, book illustrations. Children's literature is full of wonderful images, the earliest visual art introduced into young lives. Some illustrations simply do what you'd expect: illustrate the stories told in text. But many go beyond that minimum, expanding the story by including details and nuances missing in the simple language of written stories.

Anunziata (Nancy) Pignatelli, a much admired preschool teacher at Public School 110 in Greenpoint, Brooklyn, describes her school as "dedicated to educating the whole child—our motto is 'Growing Hearts and Minds'" and she sees VTS as having an integral role in working toward both goals. She says VTS questions have become so much a "part of my language I don't even have to think to use them, even at home. I find them naturally coming into play particularly when introducing books."[2]

Erin Jeanneret, who teaches at Mott Haven Academy in the South Bronx, echoes this sentiment and offers a few specifics:

I use VTS a lot during read-alouds or shared reading experiences. For instance, before reading, I have students look at the cover of a book and just say what they notice. I then restate their responses. It helps build interest in the story. I also use it when the pictures tell the stories more than the words do. I've seen how kids begin to look more in depth at the pictures when I do this for a few days.[3]

Spending more time with pictures and looking more deeply are important skills for children. They strengthen the eye-mind connection, essential exercise for their brains. They nurture understanding of the role images play in our lives: they inform us about many important things in ways that text alone cannot do. There's an old saying that "a picture's worth a thousand words," and while it's hard to compute that equation exactly, we only have to think how, while news stories reveal a lot, a whole lot more is communicated when they are accompanied by images. Reading or hearing about an earthquake is one thing, but seeing the physical and human consequences deepens the experience immeasurably—and this is especially important when we want to help students develop empathy and other social-emotional skills.

Lise White, who teaches at CNS with Carly Reagan, described a practice similar to Erin's. VTS is a part of her arsenal as she approaches books with the youngest kids at CNS, from age two through three.

I love to use VTS when book browsing with children. Rather than read, we talk our way through books. I have a child who loves to be read to, wants to be told what's in the book. I'm delighted that she loves stories, but I wonder if she's taking the easy road out. This way she doesn't have to work so hard. VTS calls all the kids into action. They have to look, think actively, speak, listen actively. It makes the whole approach to books an active experience.[4]

Most VTS-trained preschool teachers similarly rely on VTS to activate, enliven, and enrich children's experience of books. Exploring the images gives children opportunity to make meaning of what they hear, something that assists greatly with reading comprehension later. But Lise is talking about more than that: she's counting on the capacity of young children to make sense of wholes, not just parts, to engage in critical and creative thinking, something that Rosemary Agoglio refers to as honoring the child's "intelligence of vision," a paraphrase summing up the work of Rudolf Arnheim.

Rosemary was founding education director of the Eric Carle Museum of Picture Book Art, an inviting place set among the rolling landscape of central Massachusetts, on the outskirts of Amherst. Eric Carle is the much beloved author and illustrator of, for example, *The Very Hungry Caterpillar*, a book that's found its way into the hearts and minds of countless children—not to mention a few parents and others who value children's literature.[5] In 2002, together with his wife, Barbara, he founded a museum dedicated to collecting, exhibiting, and preserving the illustrations of books enjoyed by families for generations. As Rosemary puts it, the museum's mission remains, "To encourage rich connections with art beginning with images first seen in childhood . . . to create generations of museum goers."[6]

The first director of the museum, Nichols B. Clarke, suggested that Rosemary explore VTS as a means of achieving their intentions, and she quickly saw that it worked to encourage visitors of many ages to look with fresh eyes at the illustrations on exhibit, to engage in "thinking through art." While this approach met with great success for many museum visitors, the youngest, for whom so many of the books were intended, were less likely to participate in these facilitated discussions. Museum displays are hard for little ones—it's hard to see pictures hung at adult eye levels, to stand to look, to remain hushed and still. Perhaps the answer was in returning to the book, an art form that can be shared with even the youngest of children.

To address the challenges of honoring both children and books, Rosemary called on a young staff member of the museum, Megan Dowd Lambert, who had recently finished a master's degree in children's literature. Megan saw a correlation between VTS and discussion-based approaches to books that represented a major trend in early reading.

Putting various pieces together, what she developed was soon called the "Whole Book Approach." In it, the picture book is treated as "an art form by creating opportunities to discuss how the pictures, design, and production elements: format, jacket, cover, and endpapers, of the picture book interact with the text to create an artistic whole," according to the museum's website.[7] That sounds like a lot for children to appreciate, but Carly's earlier statement illustrates the sensitive way it manifests: "Rather than read, we talk our way through books."

The Carle Museum's website points out that the Whole Book Approach "shares some common ground with the American Library Association's Dialogic Reading, a technique that has shown that pausing . . . to talk about the story aids, rather than hinders, comprehension by providing time for reflection, clarification, and expansion."[8] Rosemary told me, "The museum has taken the ALA's motto—'Hear and Say Reading'—and expanded it to become 'See, Hear, and Say Reading,' in support of embracing all aspects of books and importantly nurturing both visual and verbal literacy in children." It's a productive pairing: down the road a year or two when preschoolers begin constructing meaning from written language—really reading—the ability to picture what they read greatly assists them in understanding text. Rosemary expanded on this:

> I think the important connection between VTS and the Whole Book Approach (WBA) is not only the connection between visual and verbal literacy, although that is important, but the shift in the role of the learner in both approaches, from engagement to enabling. In the WBA the shift from reading "to children" (liken this to a museum lecture tour) to reading "with children" (an opportunity for the viewer/listener to actively participate by thinking with one's eyes) engenders critical engagement with the art form of the book. Children not only make meaning of what they see in a specific book but also forge a connection to art and a lifelong approach to learning.[9]

VTS AND SCIENCE

Leaving this particular and very rich application of VTS, I want to share a few examples of others. I asked Sarah O'Leary how she had let VTS inform her teaching during recent weeks, and she sent me a raft of material:

> *We used the questions at the aquarium while watching underwater crea-*
> *tures do what they do. Kids loved it. We also did a unit on sinking and*
> *floating where the ability to have discussions was helpful. I first asked for*
> *predictions: what did they think might happen when we put different objects*
> *into a cylinder of water? We had those lists to compare to what actually*
> *happened. We also made observations about a plant that wilted and then*
> *died and about another that also wilted but recovered. What made me*
> *glad was that on each occasion I could count on the kids making many and*
> *thoughtful observations. They become small scientists. It sets up a necessary*
> *basic behavior.*[10]

Sarah also used VTS while the children were examining an incubator with duck eggs, seeking for them to notice more and to give evidence to back up their ideas.

Meanwhile, all teachers at Charlestown Nursery School, like most teachers who can, take children outside on frequent expeditions. Studying nature (seasonal characteristics, weather, and so forth) as well as the visible evidence of changes wrought by time are topics. Conveniently, Bunker Hill with its smaller version of the Washington Monument is a short walk.

The monument commemorates an early battle in the fight for American independence from England, one where it became clear both that the Colonists were woefully underprepared and that they'd fight fiercely to the end anyway. While few neighborhoods can boast monuments, most have a mix of old and new and the differences can be seen. With walks playing a central role in the school's overall plan, Erika Miles reports that VTS is in continuous play both during walks and afterward as they recall what they saw and did:

> Using VTS to notice more about the environment is a harder task than looking at images or other stationary subjects, but it's useful to have a familiar way to get children to notice more and to think about what it tells us. In fact we go back and forth between the questions "What do you notice or see?" and "What's going on here?" The noticing serves as the basis for thinking about what we can learn from thinking about what we see.[11]

One of the reasons using VTS outside is challenging is that it's hard for the children to know what to focus on, but perhaps that's a good thing. Paying attention isn't always easy; lots of distractions exist. Still, the habit of reading our natural environment, despite the challenge to focusing, is a good sensibility to develop early—not that it's hard to interest children in nature. My second grandchild is three and a half, and she has her nose to the ground a huge amount of the time she's outside. It takes forever to get to the pond near where I live if I let her be the guide—and I usually do.

One way I've used VTS with little ones is to visit a natural history museum. We can successfully discuss many dioramas (as displays of animals set in habitats are called), in part because the animals are usually involved in some kind of activity, often dramatic—story vignettes not completely different from what we find in pictures. While action is implied, the animals don't actually move, so we can examine them for a while. Some museums have portable habitats with smaller animals and birds and/or miniature ones that can be borrowed and brought to classrooms for discussion.

Many museums have areas specifically designed for younger children, and they often contain displays with live animals and insects to examine and discuss. Having something alive and real but small and contained to look at makes it easier to have discussions about some aspect of nature. In addition, having experts nearby can be useful to support what children say. Such support is especially helpful if we aren't all that sure what we're looking at.

VTS AND MATH

Sarah O'Leary also sent me tapes of using VTS adaptations in contexts where observation was essential but where becoming thoughtful observers wasn't the point of the lesson. In one, she wanted the children to continue their evolving understanding of what numbers were and what they helped us do.

The "image" to be examined was created by a sequence of towers made from Unifix cubes, present in most preschools. Cubes were stacked on top of one another to create ten towers; one cube was tower number one; two cubes, tower two; and so on. The child whose turn it was left the circle. Another child chose one tower to remove and hid it. When the turn taker returned, she or he found a pattern of nine columns and a break in the pattern where one was missing.

This kind of activity allows us to test one finding by Russian behavioral scholar Lev Vygotsky. The first is that children can accomplish unfamiliar tasks when helped by appropriate assists—for example, asking the right questions (ones that stimulate the applicable thinking) and in this case a very concrete task (find and give a number to the missing tower by counting the remaining towers).

The questions Sarah used to assist the children were familiar: What's going on with these towers? What's missing? What do you see that made you say that?

The group of towers constituted the image of the moment. The cubes were as familiar to the kids as the questions. The missing cubes created the ambiguity. As with VTS, Sarah pointed to whatever children mentioned; they were also allowed to touch and to count. Sarah paraphrased what they said.

Getting to the number of the missing tower may have taken one wrong answer, but it happened pretty fast. The child who hid the relevant tower counted out the cubes in confirmation. You could hear the satisfaction caught on tape. And with it, the children added a very concrete experience dealing with numbers in a task none of these four-year-olds could do without the assists.

A second Vygotsky finding, Sarah reminded me when we were talking about the numbers project, is in play during VTS image discussions: that new tasks may also be accomplished with help from a "more capable peer"—someone who is essentially your equal (therefore at a similar developmental level) but who is a step or two ahead in one area. The peer thinks and acts just like the person faced with the task in most ways but happens to have a leg up with regard to a particular challenge.

For example, in image-based VTS, when one child provides logical evidence to back an opinion, the child who is more idiosyncratic observes this slightly more advanced behavior. The same is true with opinions about what's happening itself: the child who thinks a group might be cutting flowers when there is no evidence of flowers listens as another says the group is playing a game, which in fact they are—though perhaps not checkers as the child suggested in the discussion of *Domino Players*. They all assist one another when they find different things to add to the reading of the image.

This is how all the children grow, something we know from evidence collected by Abigail Housen as we built VTS.

VTS IN PROBLEM SOLVING AND COMMUNITY BUILDING

I'm not ready to move on from Sarah's "laboratory for VTS in action" as I call her classroom. In a separate tape, we see another way she's adapted VTS: to discuss issues relevant to how to function within a classroom setting. In this case, she wanted the children to solve an actual dilemma: the many papers left on tables unidentified and unfinished. She knew that reminders weren't working and that getting mad was point-less, so she decided to set up a scenario to give them, first, a chance to identify the problem and, second, figure out a solution.

To give the children something to discuss, Sarah created a game. She used a set of five blocks, each with a picture of a child in the class on the side of the blocks that children could see. She animated the blocks as the story went along. At an appropriate moment, she laid a paper with some drawing on it in front of the Tom and Mary blocks. The Beth block and two others found their way off to the side as the story unfolded. She then described a scenario:

> I'm going to tell you a story. Tom and Mary are in the story, and so is Beth. During morning choices Tom and Mary were looking out the window at the construction site. "The crane is so high!" said Mary. "Oh look at the excava-tor," said Tom. "I'm going to draw it." As Tom was drawing, Beth came over and invited him to join her and others in the dramatic play area. Tom quickly dropped what he was doing and followed Beth, leaving his drawing on the table and Mary behind. So now I want you to think: what just went on here?[12]

I've pared the discussion that followed down to its basics, leaving out most of the paraphrases as well as comments that echo others—al-though all the repeats involved minor variation and showed that the children were not only listening to one another but also agreeing. (As you read, as an exercise in using VTS, try improvising paraphrases to each comment.) It's important to know that developing empathy is a regular topic within the overall program of the school.

> TAMARA: So he was playing and she came over and said, "Tom, come and play" and that hurt Mary's feelings.
>
> SARAH: So maybe a good thing was that Beth came over and asked Tom to play but maybe a tricky thing was that it might have hurt Mary's feelings. What else do we notice about this? Rosie, what did you see happen?
>
> ROSIE: Mary could just go.

RAYMOND: *Maybe Beth could ask more children.*

SARAH: *I see by your "thumbs up" that many of you agree that the problem was leaving Mary behind. So thank you. You saw something I didn't see when I set this up. It was very kind of you. Now I'm going to start this over and wonder what more you might notice.*

Though someone having hurt feelings wasn't the dilemma Sarah wanted them to address, she was pleased by the indication that discussions of feelings and empathy were being internalized. To get the children to focus on the dilemma of abandoned papers, Sarah reintroduced the problem by describing the same setup, but she told them that she'd changed the story, correcting the problem they pointed out. "This time, when Beth came over," Sarah said, "She asked both Tom and Mary to join her and others in dramatic play." Sarah also made a bit more of the fact that Tom left an unfinished drawing on the table.

SARAH: *What do you notice this time?*

ANNIE: *I notice that five are in dramatic play, so now it's full.*

SARAH: *Good counting. Dramatic play is full for now. What more?*

TOMMY: *They can't leave their spot because then if someone didn't know someone was there, they would write on their picture because they didn't know.*

SARAH: *So Tom and Mary's hard work could go home with someone else. This is the problem I was thinking of. And this is something I've noticed in our classroom. I see lots of people leaving their hard work, not putting it in the save drawers or the trash. So what could we do to fix that problem?*

TAMARA: *Another child could come over and say, "Whose work is this?"*

NATHAN: *Tom could come back and put it in the save drawer.*

SARAH: *Who thinks this is a good solution? I see most thumbs up but two that are down. Raymond, what more do you think we could do?*

RAYMOND: *Tom needs to go back to dramatic play after.*

SARAH: *Ah yes. When Tom has put his drawing in his save drawer, he then can go back and join Beth and the others. Thank you, friends. We now have ideas for what to do with our work and if we see something that's just been left.*

Sarah applied the children's experience having discussions with many contributing ideas to giving them many opportunities to express themselves. This ability becomes a common thread that weaves its way through the days and lessons.

Pulling back from the example of unsigned papers, I can easily see that VTS, used in this way, helps build a sense of how to take responsibility for one's work and also how to operate within a community, an issue about which Carly Reagan is particularly lucid. "I see one role preschool teachers have is trying to give substance to the notion of community—what it means to be part of a community," she explained to me.

> Community doesn't necessarily involve consensus. I see one aspect of it at these ages as finding different ways to move from "me" to "we." You're sitting next to me but it's okay for us to have different points of view. Friends can have different perceptions. We need to show children we understand that differences exist and we think it's okay.[13]

I'm inclined to echo that last sentiment. Differences of opinion don't necessarily undermine the essential "we" of both our local and global communities. If preschool-age children can, despite differences, develop a sense of kinship with their classmates as part of moving slowly away from the egocentrism, a necessary stage of identity development, they will be building a foundation for understanding an important aspect of living in diverse communities and, in fact, a globalized world.

VTS AND WRITING STORIES

While on the subject of adaptive uses of VTS, Meg Brown, a Charlestown Nursery School teacher who coteaches three- and four-year-olds with Carly, told me this:

> Separate from the scheduled image lessons, we use VTS to prompt storytelling. Carly and I choose a picture that connects to a theme we'd like kids to

address—for example a season. One of us facilitates the picture discussion while the other writes down what kids notice. Afterwards, we go back over the list with the children and ask them to weave these elements (and others that come up) into stories they invent as a group. We write these down as a record for the children and we also use them as pieces of evidence to help us keep track of change—assessing the journey. We might put them into kids' portfolios. Sometimes they become part of a display, a record of what they've done—and when we do this, we hang them low so kids can see and be reminded. Sometimes stories become a book that is then illustrated to share with others including parents or visitors. But even when we share a work sample, what matters to us is the process of story creation. We reflect on the process to inform what we do next.[14]

It's hard to overstate the value of this. Some children in this class have been at CNS since they were toddlers, and most have been there for two years. Incipient storytelling skills were on view in the discussion of *Le Gourmet* facilitated by Erika Miles in chapter 1—for example, in Ana's opening comment: "There's a little girl standing up and eating her porridge. She's a girl because of her hair and dress." Immediately thereafter, Charles built on that saying, "She's stirring her porridge." Other children added complicating factors about missing parents, curtains, and what might be happening in the second half of the picture, cut off as it was mid-table. These comments could be a start to the notes that Meg referred to here: they form essential elements in what could be an outline for the children to build on for a story of their own.

All the examples of VTS in action throughout the day build on behaviors that begin during the VTS image discussions: making observations, thinking about what we see tells us, drawing conclusions, articulating ideas that emerge, providing evidence—even social behaviors like taking turns and listening. These behaviors also result from the strategy having become second nature to teachers; the questions in particular have been internalized and deeply ingrained into practice. Why? Because they produce great responses from children. They honor their many capabilities, as Rosemary Agoglio of the Carle Museum wanted to see happen.

A FINAL STORY

Sometimes the VTS spin-off is not another lesson but simply mining the discussions for information they give us. Dori Jacobsohn has a wonderful story that offers a case in point.

Dori was doing a demonstration of VTS for the faculty of the University of Chicago Lab School, a private nursery school where students come from a combination of faculty and graduate students' children and of educated and generally well-off parents. She projected an image created by the French painter Henri Rousseau (see figure 3.1).[15] Rousseau taught himself to paint, and his quirky paintings were much admired by other artists of the day who appreciated his inventiveness. He painted scenes he imagined, often including settings he'd never seen

FIGURE 3.1   Henri Rousseau, *Le Douanier* (*The Sleeping Gypsy*)

(such as the one depicted, supposedly the habitat of a lion), with what he envisioned as a gypsy sleeping nearby.

The class having the following discussion included a four-year-old girl from India who was still learning English. Something about the image induced her to speak. The transcript starts with Dori's paraphrase of the preceding comment to which Soraya responds.

> DORI: *Juliet is pointing because I think that maybe she doesn't have all the words for what is in the lower right hand corner. She noticed this, maybe a vase or some kind of container. And she noticed this instrument over here and she referred to it as a guitar. Okay, Soraya, I see that your hand is up and then Lucy and then Leon.*
>
> SORAYA: *It is actually in India and they call it something else. It is not a guitar.*
>
> DORI: *So you are thinking that maybe they are in India.*
>
> SORAYA: *I know they are.*
>
> DORI: *What are you looking at that makes you say that they might be in India?*
>
> SORAYA: *'Cause in India when we are awake, they are sleeping, and when we are sleeping, they are awake.*
>
> DORI: *Okay you are thinking they are in India because they are sleeping and we are awake, so it is a different time zone.*
>
> SORAYA: *And that is called a sitar.*
>
> DORI: *And you think that this instrument might be called a sitar if they are in India. We have two ideas, it might be a guitar or it might be a sitar.*
>
> SORAYA: *It is not a guitar and there is not another word for it. It is a different instrument.*[16]

Dori added in conversation with me, "Speculating that the family calls relatives at odd hours, it is a beautiful example of learning about or observing the experiences children bring with them. This is what children do when looking: identify what they recognize from life experience." The comments also represent the concrete sureness of their thinking: the image depicts India, in Soraya's view, and therefore the instrument must be a sitar.[17]

Reasoning is often referred to as a higher-level thinking skill, but it's a skill this child employs easily. She may not be right in her conclusions, but she's nothing if not logical, one aspect of reason. She's also a four-year-old child who knows what she knows and won't be swayed. The setting may, in fact, be entirely fanciful, and the instrument might be, say, a mandolin, not a sitar, but her reasoning is impeccable.

A child who recently came to another country and has to learn everything anew, including language, might be forgiven for sitting out discussions. But given an image to discuss and the ideas of others to respond to, she's animated, forthright, and forceful. Not bad.

Before we move on to examples of learning nurtured by VTS, here's a listing of adaptive uses described in this chapter and any changes of the strategy to accommodate those uses.

AT A GLANCE: ADAPTING VTS FOR OTHER LESSONS

- VTS and books: No change of facilitation is required. All the questions apply to discussions of illustrations in books. What can be added is the Carle Museum's Whole Book Approach: occasionally, children can be asked to consider more than book covers and illustrations, but the form of the book as well: how it's made and how the insides of covers (called the endpapers) are used, for example.
- VTS and science: Use VTS questions and response mechanisms to engage children in discussions that vary from getting kids to look at what they see on walks; to studying behavior in aquariums or zoos; to making observations and predictions regarding other experiments with nature that find their way into classrooms (plants and germination experiments; unhatched eggs); to visiting natural history museums and using their displays. VTS remains a useful and familiar way to encourage looking, thinking, and sharing observations and insights that nurture the natural scientist in all children.

- VTS and math: Use tools such as Unifix cubes to create patterns and other opportunities to count, calculate, and solve a problem as a group (such as finding a missing element) using the VTS questions and facilitation process.
- VTS and social behavior: Ask students to consider classroom dilemmas and behavioral issues by way of creating a scenario that dramatizes real challenges within the classroom. Use discussion both to define the problem as the children see it and to brainstorm solutions.
- VTS and creating stories: Using a teacher partner or assistant, make notes as children talk during image discussions and use the comments as the outline for creating a story. Adding, building on, or letting them change the ideas that emerged during the discussions, write down a brainstormed story that children can illustrate with drawings. Perhaps make a book or display of the story for sharing with others, including parents.
- VTS and mining comments for personalization: Particularly if you have made tapes, listen to the comments of an assortment of children and use what they say as indicators of what they know from life, what their concerns are, what particularly interests them, what strengths emerge for you to nurture, what limits you want to help them overcome. You can compare this information to other data you pick up from parents and ongoing classroom contributions, interactions, and behavior.

CHAPTER 4

VTS Impact on Children
Charting Evidence of Growth

IN THIS CHAPTER, we focus on what we know about how children grow as result of VTS. To discern the impact, we will look at examples of children's thinking and language.

On the kind of fall day that makes Brooklyn particularly lovely—warm, clear, and sunny—Anunziata (Nancy) Pignatelli turned her class of four-year-olds over to her assistant teacher while she sat on the edge of the action with a single student, Hamad. She was armed with a reproduction of the painting seen in figure 4.1, a pencil, and paper ready to write down what Hamad said in response to a question: What's going on in the picture?[1]

Here's what he said:

Food.
Cat.
Tree.
Boy.
Clothes.
Girl.

Nancy wrote down this list of observations, noting that Hamad pointed to each thing mentioned as he went along. What he noticed constituted a reasonable inventory of what there is to see. It's not difficult to

FIGURE 4.1   Carmen Lomas Garza, *Naranjas (Oranges)*

find each though it's possible that what he saw as "cat" was one puppy among many, perhaps the offspring of the larger dog that seems to be focused on a boy beneath the tree. This exercise isn't about what an adult might see, however, but rather an attempt to gather information about exactly what Hamad saw at this point in the school year, unaided.[2]

Nancy repeated the same "hands-off" process the following April. She showed Hamad the picture again and asked the same opening question. And here's what he said this time, again pointing to what he observed, noted by his careful scribe:

> *She's giving an orange.*
> *There's a dog in the grass, there's a dog looking at grass.*
> *There's a boy in the tree.*
> *There's a man picking an orange.*
> *That dog is jumping.*
> *That dog is looking at the girl.*

Once again Hamad provided a litany of what he saw, but this time "food" became oranges," "cat" now became several "dogs," both observations more specific and more accurate than they were in the fall. Instead of single-word responses, each observation was expressed in a sentence. He located details within a scene—"there's a dog in the grass," "a boy in the tree." Importantly, he described actions—"giving an orange," a dog is "jumping" or "looking at the girl," the "boy is in the tree."

Between the two samples, five months of preschool had passed. Ten VTS discussions were included among the myriad activities over the year. Because so much else transpired, VTS cannot be credited as the sole factor in the differences between the two interviews, but it's very likely the main cause of two aspects: first, the increase in detail and specificity describing what he sees within the scene ("there's a boy in the tree" instead of just "tree" or "boy"). Second, Hamad now includes inferences ("giving an orange," "the dog is jumping," or "the dog is looking at the girl")—what I refer to as storytelling elements, albeit short ones. If these were notes for the class to use to create a story together, they'd provide great story elements.

This is a fairly dramatic example of what other samples collected by Nancy show, but the kinds of change resonate in others. For example, the opening comment of a classmate during the fall interview was "I see a grandmother giving an orange to a kid." In the second interview, the first sentence was "A girl found a fruit and she's giving the fruit to her grandma because the grandma doesn't have enough fruit." Like Hamad, this child was observant from the start though slightly more verbal than he, but the story drawn from observations went from a single, simply described interaction to a sequence of actions. She even included an unprompted *because*, providing a reason for the little girl to be handing a fruit over to her grandma.

Here's another pair of interviews that Nancy collected that year and included here in their entirety. In the fall, Sophie revealed herself to be as good an observer as Hamad. In one long sentence, she provided a list of what she saw; she also pointed to each detail as she went along:

> There's a little girl, a lady, a dog, a daddy who wants a peach, and a dog is trying to chase it, and another dog and another dog. I can even see some pants up in the tree.
>   The lady has peaches inside the april [apron?].
>   The little kid is giving the lady a peach and the lady is going to give the girl a peach.

In her second interview the following spring, Sophie's observational skill, already good, increased. We can almost follow her eyes around the picture starting at the lower left. She also drew more inferences from her observations:

> There is laundry on the lines.
> There is a cactus right next to the tree.

There is someone up in the tree picking an orange.
There's a lot of dogs playing.
  A little girl is giving her mommy an orange. She was helping her mommy
to pick oranges from the ground.

Sophie began the year with a list of observations, and by spring, she described things she saw with detail: the "laundry is on the lines." She not only noticed a cactus missed earlier, but located it in the picture as "next to the tree." An observation from interview one—"I can even see some pants up in the tree"—became the more logical "There is someone up in the tree picking an orange." The inference in this case is another example of what I call incipient storytelling, and the rest of the interview continued in this vein—dogs playing, a child helping her mother and giving her an orange in the process.

Interestingly, Erin Jeanneret, who teaches preschool at Mott Haven Academy in New York, described this same arc of development when reflecting on what she'd seen and heard over the seven years she's been using VTS at this well-reviewed charter school. She told me, "The changes I've seen over each year are students going from one- and two-word observations to more and more detailed observations and some pinpointing of what they see. By spring I see less idiosyncrasy, more grounded observations and the starts of stories."[3] By this measure, Sophie and Hamad are right on schedule.

Nora Elton has seen this development too and credits art for the story-related growth. A former art teacher, Nora has taught many grade levels and is now the mother of one five-year-old and another twenty-two-month-old child. She has acted as a volunteer VTS facilitator in two schools in East Boston, a largely Hispanic section of Boston, not far from Logan International Airport. She believes that by looking at art, the children "were able to do something that they couldn't otherwise. They become storytellers as they share their own experiences and personal connections to images." She doesn't mean they are ready to say, "Once a upon a time . . .," but that they are finding more and more snippets within pictures that they think about as if telling stories. They effectively animate what they see.[4]

Reread Sophie's second interview and pretend it's your own outline of key ideas for a story—maybe a children's book—you intend to write. How much more would it take you to create a narrative with plot, characters, setting, and action? Particularly if you mined the picture for more, which is exactly the behavior the question "What more can we find?" seeks to promote.

While we're on the topic of the behaviors you can hear in children's language by the spring of a preschool year, here's another comment, this one from a child in Sarah O'Leary's class that parallels the kind of thinking we've seen before—and a bit more as well. I've taken this comment from one of Sarah's smart phone video clips; the discussion took place in April of the year.[5]

The image the child sees, by the Mexican artist Diego Rivera, shown in figure 4.2, depicts a scene with a great deal of activity.[6] What appears to be an extended family, young and old, smash a piñata with a long

FIGURE 4.2   Diego Rivera, *La Piñata (A Christmas Tradition)*

stick and scramble for the candy that tumbles out when it's broken. In the mayhem, one person has fallen to the ground, and another figure, smaller than the rest, stands off to the side apparently in tears.

Piñatas are a traditional entertainment at Mexican birthdays, and they have become popular enough for them to be recognizable by students in Boston Chinatown, in this case. Two earlier comments in the discussion identified the piñata and spoke of the colors in the picture. Then a very excited Mateo got his turn:

> There's, um, one people that's pushed right there and one that's crying. 'Cause either one didn't get a bat and the other one got pushed and they're not being respectful because not showing focus and respecting . . . it's not safe to do that. And someone wasn't hurt. Or, or, or not sharing. And that's not, not empathy and they're not supposed to do that.[7]

This comment provides us with a sample of Mateo's insightful thinking about what he noticed, and it's also a fairly typical example of preschool language ability: the complexity and breadth of the ideas are slightly ahead of the ability to express them. This phenomenon is far from uncommon, and not just with preschoolers. Nonetheless, he conveyed his message.

SOCIAL AND EMOTIONAL GROWTH

I'll return to the topic of children's language, but for the moment it's important to acknowledge that Mateo has a keen eye and a big heart. The discussion had started off with the usual instruction to take a moment to look left to right, up to down, and to take in the whole scene. We can tell Mateo followed the instruction thoroughly. He seems to have noticed and thought about a lot, and in his comment, he tells the class what stands out for him, both the man on the ground in the front and the crying child who's off to the right side. He seems genuinely concerned with the predicaments of both characters: one who's been treated roughly and the other denied a turn. He states that pushing isn't okay and that not getting a turn can make you feel bad.

In terms of visual meaning making, Mateo's comments show that he doesn't simply notice but easily draws inferences from what he sees and reads the implications of positions and gestures. He creates mini narratives within an overall story of a group battering a piñata, something mentioned in a comment that preceded his. Remarkably, he even suggests a sequence of events. The fallen character was pushed during the fracas and another was denied a turn with the bat, resulting in tears.

Both the observations and his interpretations are a far cry from the minimal and idiosyncratic observations that were the norm in Mateo's class in December. Please flip back to chapter 1 and reread the discussion of *Domino Players*. It will give a sense of the midpoint between their starting place in visual meaning making and the predictable changes that occur over a year of preschool. Mateo's comments represent what is well within reach; such changes are also apparent in the discussion of *Le Gourmet*.

This comment, however, contains information about more than ability to read pictures. Sarah has strong evidence that other lessons are sinking in: in this case, the learning that has stuck is the result of frequent discussions of empathy and thoughtful dispute solving. Mateo even remembers the vocabulary and understands what it means. They have become part of how he thinks. Sarah had other evidence that these ideas had taken root when students found a problem in the sample discussion in chapter 3 where the children felt bad that Mary had been left behind when Beth issued an invitation to Tom alone.

Listening to children talk during VTS discussions provides a venue for seeing what children have internalized of the array of information and experience offered at school and from life in general during these precious years. Children at these ages are wonderfully receptive to learning; I think of them as sponges and have a great example watching my three-and-a-half-year-old granddaughter take in and use everything she hears, usually for better, sometimes not so much. Carly Reagan, from CNS, offers a reflection on why VTS itself aids with dispute settlement and other social communication. "VTS practice teaches how to deal with conflict," she told me. She continued:

> In a VTS lesson we count on the fact that we all look at the same picture, but see it differently from one another. The way the facilitator paraphrases the children's observations models acceptance and democracy. All responses are equally valid. And there is always more to find and think about.
>
> Two things are at work here, even in circumstances where you feel you're right about something. The fact of hearing evidence—the requirement to explain—seems to make dissension easier to handle.
>
> This form of discussion and debate tends to build an atmosphere easing other discussions. Productive discussions don't deteriorate into frustration. As long as personal feelings are allowed but not to dominate, interpreting material stays more easily open.[8]

Lise White, Carly's CNS colleague who teaches the toddlers, adds other valuable insights into the ways VTS contributes to the development of positive social interactions:

> Children who are at first hesitant about participating get to practice speaking in front of their peers. Children who are confident speaking in groups learn to listen to each other and cede the floor to others. The lessons develop self-regulation and self-control, fostered through sitting and looking together without speaking and then taking turns. Focus develops as we look ever more closely and deeply at the picture, tuning out other distractions.
>
> I also use linking and divergence to scaffold perspective taking. Understanding that someone else thinks the same as you do about something, and someone else thinks differently than you do, is a set of important life skills that children can begin to learn as soon as they enter group settings. Learning to disagree civilly is one of the most important skills school can foster in young children. Also, practicing VTS over time tends to breed the notion that differing ideas can coexist, even in one's own head.[9]

PARTICIPATION: WHAT ENCOURAGES IT?

I wanted to know why teachers thought children who are normally quiet speak up during VTS, as Lise mentioned. We've heard about this phenomenon since the early days of testing VTS. Carly Reagan began her answer with a single word, *predictability*:

> *Knowing the questions and what was expected seems to make all comfortable with participating. They know what to do. They are less likely to feel "on the spot." I think another factor might be that they're not looking toward one another but focused on the topic of conversation, the picture. I think for the moment they can feel as if they are just talking to their teacher who is going to support them.*
>
> *I actually think VTS aids the performance of all children. But it might particularly show up when they are accustomed to another looking protocol we use: see, think, wonder. I've also seen greater willingness to start right in with kids who had VTS experience as toddlers.*[10]

Many people think that a big reason for wide participation is that the subject matter is images. Erin Jeanneret spoke about an incident in which a child who was very reluctant to speak came alive when the right picture came along:

> *VTS was particularly helpful with one child who was shy to the point that we weren't clear what was going on. She would raise her hand during VTS discussions but at first was unable to say what she had in mind. But looking at one picture, she raised her hand and said, "I see three dogs." From then on she shared regularly.*[11]

Most teachers have similar stories to relate. Nancy Pignatelli of PS 110 in Brooklyn took to VTS in the first place because she herself loves art and enjoyed an opportunity to fold it into her teaching. An element of VTS that particularly pleases her is the fact that the kids enjoy it as much. "I love the kids' reactions to pictures as they are shown," she told me.

> One child entered school with delayed speech, and at first I thought it was an issue of English as second language. He was also very shy and rarely said anything. During our third VTS discussion, he raised his hand and spoke. It seemed to be the arena for him to develop both language ability and confidence. VTS enabled him to become himself. And the good news was it spilled over into other class activities.[12]

Nancy echoed other teachers when mentioning one of the advantages she saw in terms of positive social behaviors. She also summarized growth over the year in a similar way:

> It's not so easy for my kids to disagree in most contexts, but they are very easy with it during VTS. Their comments may start with one or two words, but by midyear, I hear narratives developing. I recently saw them develop three different scenarios, and they seemed to know they could coexist.[13]

What Nancy mentioned about her suspicion that her very quiet child spoke another language at home is often the case. Children for whom English is a second language often sit back, watch, and listen, at least during initial VTS discussions. But once they make their first comment, they are hooked and in most cases are less reluctant to speak up in other classes too.

Why? Probably for some of the same reasons that reticent kids contribute: predictability, the fact that everybody is looking at the images, not so much each other, and that they don't feel as if they are required to come up with the right answer, not to mention saying it correctly. I think another reason is witnessing how the teacher behaves: listening without judgment and responding even-handedly to everyone, for example. Moreover, through the pointing, the children see the teacher understands them. Through the paraphrase, they hear their thoughts expressed in English, including vocabulary in the likely case that they are missing key words. They also know the teacher has made an effort to acknowledge them and that feels good. They have accomplished a task just like their classmates.

Of equal importance is the fact that VTS discussions focus on stories told in pictures instead of writing. The children can look and find the elements that interest them and share their ideas; they tell the story. Through the exchange with the teacher, they can associate what they see with the language related to it. They also listen to their peers contributing ideas, with the authority of teacher and author removed this time. It's empowering. And given how easily they absorb what they see and hear, chances are that they remember. We could hear that in Mateo's comment; although he is a native English speaker, words like *empathy* have become part of his language.

CNS, like many nursery schools, accepts children as young as two and a half, and they can stay until they enter kindergarten, therefore having as many as three years of VTS experience. Kay Cutler also has that opportunity at the Fishback Center for Early Childhood Education in Brookings, South Dakota, a demonstration/laboratory nursery school at South Dakota State University. Children can attend the school beginning at fifteen months, and they are grouped with others up to twenty-two months. Again, as is usually the case with nursery schools, the multiage groupings maintained throughout the span that children remain at the Fishback Center increase the opportunity for peer learning.

Furthermore, children who remain for two or three years provide a longer view of their growth over time. This sometimes plays out in delightful ways. Kay and her colleagues have noted something I refer to as the "indelibility of images": a picture you've spent time examining and thinking about is hard to get out of your head. Kay remembers a conversation children had in the toddler group that was still fresh for them when they were three-year-olds. In the same way that books can be read again and again, pictures can be recycled, and one image revisited for three-year-olds was an imaginary jungle scene concocted by the naïve French artist Henri Rousseau who also painted the image of the lion that one child thought was in India, *Le Douanier (The Sleeping Gypsy)*. In the painting Kay refers to, a round orange object was repeated many times, and in one case, it sits right in front of a monkey's muzzle. As two-year-olds, two children had a debate similar to the one about gender that we read earlier. In this instance, the conversation went back and forth, one arguing that the orange disc was an orange and the other that it was the monkey's nose. Both children were sure they were right.

Much to Kay's surprise, the children recalled the conversation as three-year-olds when they looked at the picture again. Shortly after the discussion began, the same orange shape was mentioned though this time evidence was given for the different opinions: "I think it's this because . . ." And then remarkably, the girl turned to her teacher who was sitting next to her and said, "You know he and I disagreed before too, and having different thoughts is okay," Kay commented. "I'm hoping this lasts, but it seems by age three these children had learned that reasonable people can disagree."

> *Because we often have children for several years, we see the benefits of incubation, seeing behaviors mature and deepen over time. Our four- and five-year-olds will give evidence in many situations, but that's only one habit that carries. Another is that all kids know that everyone has thoughts and ideas that are worth hearing. VTS teaches them that they can share ideas and that spending more time is worth it. One day before doing a VTS session, a five-year-old boy asked, "Which pictures are we looking at today?" I was standing in the hallway outside his room with the pictures, so I turned them around and showed him the images. He replied, "Hey, I've been thinking about our discussion of this image last year and I have more to say about it!" I replied with a smile, "Great! I want to hear it."[14]*

SKILL DEVELOPMENT

Carly's three- and four-year-olds also show expansions of skills as well as the transfer of certain behaviors. One important behavior is the ever-increasing tendency to find stories within images. Equally as exciting is another behavior she's observed. "Especially when CNS has had the children since toddlers, we see them drop the notion of finding something specific when looking at other sorts of things. In many lessons we ask directive questions but that doesn't stop open-ended explorations, a habit built by way of VTS."[15]

Speaking of children who were in what CNS calls its preschool class—three- and four-year-olds who will go to kindergarten the next year—Erika Miles shared, "The first time a particular class did VTS together, some of the children had seen and discussed the picture the previous year. One of them mentioned it but the most interesting part was how this year they made a story out of what they saw. As the year went on, the responses got even more detailed and elaborate."[16]

It's impossible to make definitive claims about how and how much VTS affects children's language development. We don't have enough hard data. However, the examples I've shared give a good picture of what teachers witness. Children work to understand and communicate about images, and this effort adds to how they think and what they say. The thinking shifts result from mining more and more pictures for meanings and doing it with peers facilitated by teachers and stimulated by the right questions.

One-word observations become more detailed.

Observations that start out as isolated mentions—like items on a list—slowly but surely contain more description.

Almost as soon as this increase in detail begins, children start inferring meaning based on those observations.

At this point, many are able to supply evidence to back up their inferences.

Part of what is happening cognitively—shifts in thinking—has implications for language.

Where we first see one-word statements, we soon see the addition of some descriptive language.

When students routinely draw inferences from what they see, it pretty much requires a sentence simply to share them.

The sentences become complex when the children add their evidence.

Let's return to Mateo's comment about the piñata picture:

There's, um, one people that's pushed right there and one that's crying. 'Cause either one didn't get a bat and the other one got pushed and they're not being respectful because not showing focus and respecting . . . it's not safe to do that. And someone wasn't hurt. Or, or, or not sharing. And that's not, not empathy and they're not supposed to do that.

Let's analyze his thinking and language. He observed two people at the edges of the throng and inferred that one has fallen and another is crying. To explain what he saw, he used a sentence with two clauses: the first, "one people that's pushed" and the second, "one that's crying." Without being asked, he elaborated by explaining what happened: one has been treated disrespectfully and pushed and the other is unempathetically denied his turn with a bat. Though it's extremely doubtful that Mateo is conscious of his thinking process, he has given us a great example of advances in thinking that drive language toward greater complexity.

Sarah paraphrased his ideas but kept it at that; she didn't comment on the language though she had that information to file away. Here's her paraphrase:

Do you remember the last artwork we looked at and we saw someone on the ground and you wondered if they had been pushed? Well, Mateo noticed that there was someone in the front who's fallen down, and he wondered if maybe he had been pushed, and he also noticed that there was another person over here on the right side who was crying, maybe because he didn't get a turn. And that's inappropriate and not showing empathy.[17]

Let's remember that the purposes of paraphrasing are many—acknowledging a comment, making sure that all are aware of what's been added to their conversation and modeling syntax, for example. As teacher, you are trying to reward and bolster participation and help children understand what they have done. For purposes of thinking about this example, here's another possible way to paraphrase Mateo's comment:

Okay, Mateo, you've seen a lot in this scene, and two things that stand out for you are that one person seems to have fallen and another might be crying. You gave us your reasons: one might have been pushed—and that's not respectful behavior—and the other could be sad because he's not been given a turn. Both of these things are things we think a lot about in this class.

In both cases, look at how many words it took to restate the complexity of all he said. He had VTS since the beginning of the year, and I'd say he learned a lot about looking at pictures, and it all has consequences for his language. He has so many thoughts that words come flooding from his mouth.

The importance of responding is hard to measure, but if there is one thing about which scholars of language development agree, it's the fact that learning language is a matter of hearing and speaking with both adults and other children. Returning to cite the wisdom of Lauren Resnick and Catherine Snow,

Typically, three-year-olds are just trying to figure out how to express themselves and understand their place in the world. Four-year-olds are better

at it. They can say what they want, when and why. Just a year's practice makes them more skilled at talking things through for the sake of friendships. That said, all *preschoolers still need plenty of language support from caring, capable adults. . .*

Language is becoming a tool for explaining their world, getting things done, sharing stories, and talking about books. Preschool caregivers and teachers, then, should use their words carefully, with the constant awareness that they have a crucial responsibility to help develop oral language. . . . Teachers and caregivers should watch for opportunities to develop preschoolers' talking skills.[18]

Snow and Resnick in their book for teachers about language development beginning in preschool, *Speaking and Listening for Preschool Through Third Grade*, share a great deal of advice and insight as well as many practical suggestions for making talk happen. Snow teaches in the Harvard University Graduate School of Education, and Resnick is a distinguished University Professor of Learning Sciences and Education Policy at the University of Pittsburgh; together and alone they've spent decades helping teachers become aware of the crucial nature of conversation in the classroom.

Their thinking is worth including here because preschoolers are at an enormously important time of their lives, and much of what happens now will affect outcomes later. Similarly, what doesn't happen also has implications for the future. While I believe that humans, with the right help, can remedy all sorts of delays and setbacks, I also think that stimulating the very fertile brains of children in early childhood—given their sponge-like ability to absorb—is essential. As VTS shows, they are fully equipped for find-and-tell stories, crucial aspects of language development.

Language fluency is not a matter of knowing words and grammar but of being able to communicate effectively in varied situations. Speaking to this issue, here's one of the summary statements Jerome Bruner makes as he's ending his scholarly book on language development, *Child's Talk: Learning to Use Language:*

> *Whatever else language is, it is a systematic way of communicating to others, of affecting their and our own behavior, of sharing attention, and of constituting realities to which we then adhere just as we adhere to the "facts" of nature.*[19]

In other words, we talk to each other in ways we both understand in order to affect behavior; for example, "I want to tell you something, and I want you to listen to me and show that you do." We also talk to get on the same page with one another and set expectations to which we both adhere. Communication, though learned, is as natural as bundling up when it's cold.

Earlier in his book, Bruner writes,

> *The development of language, then, involves two people negotiating. Language is not encountered willy-nilly by the child; it is shaped to make communicative interaction effective—fine tuned . . . [It] may depend on prior social and conceptual experience.*[20]

Bruner reminds us that children learn when the time is right and the necessary foundation is in place. They do so in order to talk *to* others, and they do it *by* talking to others. The systematic aspects of language— such as correct terminology and comprehensible grammar—are learned as children try to make themselves understood; rules aren't drummed into their consciousness but learned in context. Learning to communicate is therefore a two-way proposition. Teaching language is a matter of structuring experience to include genuine give-and-take.

VTS is a setup to make communication happen. Look again at the three discussions in chapter 1. Notice that when the right subject is chosen and an inviting question is asked, children easily and quickly contribute observations. Remember that the first discussion—the one led by Dori Jacobsohn—was a "first-time" experience for the students. These beginning experiences are necessary to get to a more complex form of thinking, the one emphasized in the earlier quote from Resnick and Snow: storytelling.

Within a few months of more-or-less weekly discussions, most children are not simply observing but inferring actions from what they see. This is what I've called "incipient storytelling." These next two examples will look familiar to you: "They are eating" and "It looks like, um, the people, um, I think they are, um, cutting flowers." Admittedly, these are very short stories, but nonetheless they represent the beginnings of storytelling at a level appropriate for preschoolers.

Looking back at the first discussion, you can see how Sarah paraphrased these narrative comments—for example, "Rosie thought they might be eating food, but you think they, maybe they are cutting flowers." She stressed the kids' ideas as much as their words. She used language common to stories they read. She thus supported the storytelling while she made it easier for all to follow each comment. Through linking comments, she helped build awareness of how ideas mesh together.

Erika Miles, of CNS, eloquently summarizes the purposes served by paraphrasing, referring to her experience facilitating:

> After repeated opportunities using VTS to look at an image, children will use language and new vocabulary words that have been discussed or paraphrased by a teacher. Words that come to mind are foreground and background, but also their use of more elaborate sentences, where children will provide evidence of a theory or create a fantasized story line. Teachers try to speak to the children using, for lack of a better word, "real" language (e.g., wound instead of boo boo) and after hearing these terms repeatedly, children will incorporate that language into their own vocabulary.[21]

Although it feels something like an awful pun, let's close this chapter on VTS impact with a few stories. Kay Cutler told me that most of the Fishback Center's non-English speakers come as the children of graduate students attending the university from abroad. She considers VTS a vehicle for them learning English because of its "many anchors: looking, talking with a group of other children, pointing, paraphrasing that provides vocabulary set in context." She went on:

> We had a five-year-old non-English-speaking child fascinated by dinosaurs. He found one or more in every picture, giving him a reward for looking. At first he could barely contribute more than pointing and the single word. After three or four lessons, he began to add adjectives, and was soon off and running. It's very common that vocabulary is picked up and then used as a result of VTS conversations.[22]

Kay's colleague on the faculty of the Teaching, Learning, and Leadership Department at South Dakota State University, Mary Moeller, talks about what she's seen as how VTS encourages cognition so natural to children that it "becomes habitual and is transferred from one subject to another especially with images they come upon in other lessons. They know how to digest images. They know they have meaning." She continued:

> One story illustrates the way that students participate at different levels, some of which make VTS impact difficult to document. For example, one child remained attentive during discussions but rarely commented himself. Because his parents were friends, I found out that, at home, he spoke excitedly and in detail about what happened in VTS discussions. It would be hard to know that from what we witnessed in the preschool. But not talking doesn't mean children are not gaining. Things are firing in their brains; it's just hard to see and document. It's just lucky that I know the parents and therefore learned about this.

Another story speaks to the ways that this habit of thinking becomes an aspect of the kids' identity and this one is about a child who attended Fishback preschool and then went onto a local kindergarten.

His mother (a teacher herself) comes in to read aloud to students. As she was about to turn the page after finishing the text, her son jumped up and said, "No, we're not done." Before his mother could respond, he stood by the book and started "VTSing" with his classmates, even asking the second question. He apparently thinks of himself as a teacher, and VTS gave him a tool he found a necessary companion to the reading of a book. He was so comfortable he stepped up to lead because his mother didn't quite get it.[23]

But he did. And it seems most kids do.

CHAPTER 5

VTS and Teachers

What Do Teachers Tell Us?

THIS CHAPTER IS ABOUT what teachers have come to understand about VTS and the advice they have for those learning it. The chapter opens with what is essentially a pep talk: a sampling of teacher reviews.

The indefatigable Anna Miller directs two nursery school programs at Wayne State University in Detroit: one, the College of Education Early Childhood Center, and the other, the Merrill Palmer Skillman Institute Early Childhood Center. Beginning in 2011, she oversaw a three-year implementation of VTS in the many classrooms of both. Each year she asked for reflections from the teachers, and I've stolen bits of what they said to share with you:

I love listening to the background knowledge and personal experience children reveal when talking about a painting. There is always something else to be learned.

As a teacher, VTS has helped me with my conflict resolutions skills and asking open-ended questions. And I find myself using it at home with my grandchildren.

It allows the teacher to gain a deeper understanding of where the child is with social skills, confidence, and knowing what or how they see things. It builds confidence in the teacher's public speaking. It gives the teachers a feeling of success because they can see the children using things they learned coming out in conversations.

I was very shy and I think this helps children like me.

I think both teachers and children learn to appreciate how others' ideas can enhance their own, or even encourage them to clarify their own ideas if they disagree.[1]

These Detroit teachers appreciated many similar qualities in VTS, noting that some of the benefits serve both children and adults: "Teachers 'defend' the right of a child to express their own opinion to other children and help children not to judge . . . Personally it has helped me recognize others' opinions with more patience and tolerance." It's always encouraging to hear that once VTS gets under their skin, teachers adopt some of the behaviors expected of children as their own, maybe without noticing. It's far from rare to hear that VTS drifts home with teachers. Sometimes this has a funny side effect. I've heard the children of teachers moan, "Are you going to VTS me AGAIN?"

What's interesting among the comments was that none expressed reservations. Anna's original hope has become a reality: VTS has become ingrained in the schools' cultures and the teachers' values. It remains an official part of the Centers' programs four years after the end of the official project.

SOME CHALLENGES OF LEARNING VTS

Remaining Neutral

The Detroit experience doesn't mean everyone loves VTS; it just means that even skeptics learn to see more advantages than the opposite. And in truth, VTS practice involves challenges, some of them summed up well by another teacher familiar to you:

It's challenging to abandon the aspects of teaching that have to do with right and wrong answers and the teacher's role as information provider.

As Carly Reagan says here, VTS tests teachers even in classrooms where respect for children is paramount, as I've seen is the case at

Charlestown Nursery School where Carly teaches the three- and four-year-old live wires. She explains further:

> Though VTS fits with other hallmarks of the school's principles—such as not validating one child at the expense of others and making sure that all kids are seen as having equal value—it is still sometimes hard to remain neutral when seeking "right" answers. VTS makes it easy to keep the field level but it is challenging to maintain the same neutrality when the rules of the game go back to right and wrong. And it is definitely a challenge within VTS not to get excited about the comment of a child who rarely shares; you want to reward and validate their participation. It's difficult to navigate how to best handle that. We're not robots, we get excited too![2]

Fortunately, I know from my own life how hard it is to relinquish a commitment to rewarding exceptional behavior and to leading students to find what I want them to know. I had spent twenty-five years teaching about art in more conventional ways when I tried to adapt to the rigors of this VTS way of teaching. I did so because data told me that despite the fact that I easily engaged students, the impact stopped there. They weren't learning what I taught. It didn't stick. My goal was to enable them in ways that sent them down the road toward self-sufficiency, capable of using what I taught and of moving beyond these lessons on their own. It just wasn't happening. One thing that ubiquitous testing has shown is that this phenomenon—teaching without learning—is far from uncommon.

Of course, that isn't good news, but the insight prompted me to team up with cognitive scholar Abigail Housen to create VTS.

We were determined to make teaching that did stick:

- teaching that enabled participants to know how to approach and probe the complexities that abound in their lives
- teaching that used discussion to transform observations and ideas into shared communication
- teaching that went from initial exposure to new subjects to the beginnings of understandings

While, over years of testing VTS, we found that the learning did stick and even transferred to other situations (like the Detroit teachers report), we also observed that the differences between VTS and conventional teaching made for a number of stresses.

So, of course, I understand what Carly's talking about. It's hard to curb your enthusiasm when something unexpectedly wonderful happens! I experienced the same discomfort. I had to ask myself: "What's the point? Why do I think it's better *not* to effuse over special effort?" I thought about this as I tested VTS and eventually came to understand supportive feedback in a new way.

Here's how I'd express this way of thinking: in VTS, we consistently reward all children by listening and honoring what they say, making sure that others hear what they've contributed—whether it's one word or a long sentence, whether it seems on point or off the wall. We respond to all in the same way: those for whom participation is easy and those who tend to hang back.

Remaining neutral like this doesn't mean leaving out excitement and warmth. It means giving everyone equal respect and support, like all children deserve. Later in the day, you can always give an extra thank you to a child you know struggles. But singling out one child in front of others might even be counterproductive. Saying something like "I'm so glad you decided to share with us today" could simply serve as a reminder that this child hasn't responded before. Most kids want to be on an equal footing with peers, not exceptional in any direction, but especially if they could possibly think less of themselves because they hadn't spoken up.

We adults want to say "bravo" to each new accomplishment, but does this serve the positive reinforcement we intend? Home life is not the same for all kids, for sure, but many get all sorts of kudos for everything they do. Even three-year-olds are capable of attitude, I'd say, given the dismissive looks I've seen more than once from my now three-and-a-half-year-old granddaughter. I think praise happens so often that it means little or nothing.

Rather than feeling as if some behavior is special, I think children just want to be recognized to be as capable as they are. They want your full attention more than the repetition of "Good job!" My ten-year-old granddaughter expects her cooking to work; she just rolls her eyes if I gush. She wants honesty; the proof of the pudding is in the eating, as the saying goes.

Let's go at this a different way and return to Tamara's earlier comment about *Domino Players* in chapter 1: "It looks like, um, the people, um, I think they are, um, cutting flowers." It's easy for us to see they aren't. They're not eating either, as Rosie had contributed a minute or so earlier. If we were trying to get the children to see what actually is depicted in the picture (several things including a game of dominos), we might want to correct them. Instead, we want them to learn to apply what they know from life to describe and make sense of what they see. After all, the experience they bring (however much or little) is what they have to use on anything new to them. Support them when they make an effort.

Supporting children is the bigger point of VTS, appreciated by the veteran VTS teachers who led us into this chapter. Sure, they could say, very gently, "Not really," but in VTS we want to reward talking and sharing ideas; we want to thank children for speaking up and applying what they know to new situations. We want to hear what they notice, what they care about; through their comments, we have an important window into each child's language and thinking. Moreover, we must give them opportunity to talk if we want them to learn language; if they don't talk, they don't learn. Meanwhile, we don't learn as much as we need to know about them.

If Sarah O'Leary were seeking the right answer to what's in the picture, what would she say to Nathan who thought the group might be playing checkers? He's right that they are playing a game; it's just not checkers. He had his reason too: white dots. He just thought that checker pieces had dots, not dominos. These games are often packaged in the same box. The confusion is natural. It would take him seconds to learn the difference the next time the box came out.

Do you think Nathan would have bothered to speak if it weren't for Sarah choosing to respond to all neutrally instead of saying, however nicely, "No cigar?" when she hears an answer that's off base? Instead, she embraces the fact that they've contributed something new, "Ah! So you have a different idea . . ." She prioritizes sharing new thoughts, signaling that there can be more than a single way of perceiving and it's okay. I'm glad you've spoken and found language to express an idea, she tells the child—and given Tamara's *ums*, it looks as if she struggled a bit to spit it out.

I think of VTS as providing authentic, supportive feedback for contributing, more meaningful than what have become, through repetition, empty words of praise. And if you implement VTS over the course of preschool, however many years that is, you'll see a decrease in the idiosyncrasy as it gives way to more accurate readings of what children discuss.

Thinking About Right and Wrong Answers

I've been skirting the issue, but now let's think about Carly's second quandary: the challenge posed by moving from VTS back to right-wrong lessons, a more frequent challenge now than it used to be. Preschools were once oriented around social skills, introductions to resources, to what there is to know, to discoveries, and of course, play and fun. Now they are expected to lay ground for various academic skill sets at the expense of some emphases that were standard not so long ago.

For decades we have learned, learned to teach, and taught in the context of a dominant paradigm for teaching and learning: the domain of "right and wrong answers and the teacher's role as information provider," as Carly succinctly put it. VTS seems very different, and it is; it's a different structuring of teaching with slightly different goals. I say "slightly" because all educators, no matter what approach governs their teaching choices, want to see children grow to reach their potential and succeed in the world as result. What we differ about is how to do that.

In VTS, children can say anything that comes to mind, and the teacher remains nonjudgmental. But let's not forget that second question! Sarah posed it to Tamara phrased this way: "What do you see that makes you think they are cutting something?" Tamara's answer: "Because they have to cut flowers to keep them growing." I doubt that Sarah expected that response, and it doesn't refer back to evidence in the picture, but it comes from Tamara's memories of life around her. My guess is that she has seen a parent trim the stems of flowers after they've been in a vase a few days to keep them growing, or at least extend their life. Regardless, Sarah gamely rephrased Tamara's evidence: "So you are thinking that maybe they would have to cut the flowers to keep them growing." Would it serve well to disregard this four-year-old child's effort? What good would have been done to say, "No, Tamara, you don't see any flowers here"?

Posing the second question reminds all the students that one rule of the VTS game is to back up comments with visual evidence. Sarah's class was only a few months into VTS when they had this discussion, and it's not a hard-and-fast rule either to ask or to seek an answer to the question this early in the process. More exposure during the next few months to hearing it—and to hearing peers answer it—leads to comfort with the task that in turn leads to less idiosyncrasy.

When teachers use VTS with toddlers, they sparingly introduce this question, and when it's done, it's because a teacher thinks a child is ready to think that way. But Tamara is four, and within a few more months, she's likely to sound like her classmate Mateo building in her reasons as she makes a comment. She's ready.

Yes, during VTS discussions, children can say anything that comes to mind, but it's not a free-for-all because of that second question. The habit of providing evidence is usually thought of as a higher-level thinking skill, but when taught this way—asking for visual evidence within a picture right in front of the children—it is clearly within reach of most preschool-age people within a few months of VTS practice. This is true particularly when the children who are slightly ahead of their peers provide examples, an appropriate assist as Vygotsky might say. And once this lesson is learned at this tender age, it doesn't take much to keep it in place. If later schooling builds on this practice of supplying evidence, it will serve them well meeting standards later and in many real-life settings.

As I see it, because of the second question—and this is arguable, like virtually everything else—VTS operates at an intersection between open-endedness and right-wrong teaching.

One objective of this book is to entice you to find your own arguments regarding claims such as that and to do so because of teaching VTS and then stepping back to reflect on what you've witnessed. At the end of this chapter, I list some questions for you to assist this "practice and reflection" process as you go from discussion to discussion. My intent is to enable you to give VTS a try in your own settings and to both enjoy and learn from the process.

Learning VTS

How do you get comfortable with VTS and perform it in a way that best helps children? Dori Jacobsohn has some relevant counsel for us.

Dori has a great deal of experience teaching children and training teachers (such as those in Detroit) in VTS. To share VTS with others, she demonstrates it faithfully; for those learning without a trainer, online video clips show how different teachers do it. You can gain access to samples of teachers teaching at www.watershed-ed.org.[3] She also needs to be prepared to lead discussions that address teachers' questions about the method.

Though there is some consistency to what gives teachers pause, Dori and other trainers can never predict exactly what's going to be asked when exploring VTS. Therefore, we've all found that best practice is turning any question around: so how might we answer that? What can we figure out as a group by thinking about it ourselves? Teachers sometimes groan and beg, "Just tell me already . . ." And Dori can answer questions, of course, but she knows the learning is much more likely to stick when it's the product of the teachers' efforts. On this subject, Meg Brown from the Charlestown Nursery School told me, "As a favorite teaching artist says at the start of his workshops: 'The knowledge is in the room.'"[4]

When you are learning VTS on your own, it's not quite like having other teachers to share insights and ideas with when you want to noodle through a question. But you can do it yourself. "The knowledge is within you," to paraphrase Meg's artist friend. Many teachers across the globe have successfully done so with no expert to turn to for answers.

I recently met an example: Jacqueline (Jackie) Chung, the Senior Principal and Academic Director of St James' Church Kindergarten in Singapore. She chanced upon VTS while using the Internet creatively, thought it had merit, experimented with it in her university methods courses, and figured out not only how to do it but also how to share what she learned with others.

What's Jackie's magic? She had the willingness and took the time to ponder both her own questions and those of her students and come to understandings that worked for them. She may or may not have drawn exactly the conclusions I have, but the issue isn't what I think. It's what works for her and her colleagues—tailored to a cultural context that is both like and dissimilar to our own. Teachers at her preschool have been using VTS for eight years longer than anywhere else I know of. Remember, Singapore is one of those places cited in news stories about how systems in other countries outachieve the United States.

Meg Brown understands learning to use VTS. Here's some of her advice:

> It's worth it simply to dive in. The benefits to children include the practice of sharing, using language, becoming empowered, having your voice respected, knowing that what you say has a purpose and will be respected. My counsel to a new teacher is while you're doing it let the rhythm flow. Don't stop the momentum. You can explore some meaty topic that comes up later.
>
> What's hard to learn however is to hold back on the instinct not to steer the kids in any direction. You don't want to give too much away despite what you might know and despite what you perceive as misunderstandings. Leave VTS as a child's experience. Later you can go back and revisit a subject if you feel you have bypassed a teachable moment.[5]

You don't have to be perfect right out of the gate. Give yourself time. And pay attention. The point is, "What can I learn from thinking about what I see?" Figure out what you can learn about you and your facilitation skills and about how your students respond. Pay special attention to paraphrasing as a source of insights.

Thinking About Paraphrasing

Dori speaks to the desireability of paraphrasing well:

> VTS is fantastic for aiding kids with language development, because it combines two essential behaviors—naming what is seen and hearing how vocabulary is used in communication. However I would also add this stipulation: it's up to the teacher both to see and seize the opportunity provided.
>
> Seeing the chance is a matter of being 100 percent present so that you not only identify what the child mentions but also grasp the gist of what they are trying to say. If you're not familiar with an image, finding the parts that interest the children can take too much time, and it's often small details they zero in on. You want to be right with them.[6]

It's essential not to waste any time as you search for something you didn't expect—which is possible at any moment. Examine the pictures you choose as preparation for a discussion. Facilitating with efficiency is part of becoming a thoughtful practitioner. You might still need help finding something and have to ask a child to show you as Sarah did with the mysterious crown in the discussion of the *Domino Players*. As much as possible, you want to know the image well enough to quickly find the diverse observations that come up.

Advanced planning by looking at the images also gives you time to think about your own ways of describing what you see, what you think about it, and how you'd express your opinions. You arm yourself with language. This is not to say that you'll use it, exactly, because you don't know what children will say, and what stands out for them is often different from what you notice. Still, you don't want to make the children wait while you search the picture, struggle for words, or fall back on repeating what they say just because you aren't prepared. However, repeating is always possible if all other words fail to come to you.

Dori continues addressing the problem for teachers:

> *Teachers' own language skills are sometimes taxed as they try to paraphrase a thought that's more complex than they're used to hearing from children. Getting good at paraphrasing is way to develop a skill, but missing a chance to help a child is something to watch for: teachers' limitations should not limit kids' potential.*[7]

An unpredictable advantage to teaching VTS is that it often helps us develop our own language flexibility and the richness of the vocabulary we use. I'm not suggesting we use three-dollar words with preschoolers, but if you can respond to "I see a crown" with, "Ah so, Leilia counted these pointed shapes, and it reminds her of a crown," as Sarah did, you give Leilia a way to think about what she's seen as well as model a way to say it. Although we cannot predict that she will later adopt such language, only a few minutes later Thomas did so: "I see that there are shapes up there so those could be a car." Sarah's paraphrase of Leilia set in motion one further comment about shapes even if it was expressed in other words: Eric's comment, "I think that's fire . . . because it has these lines like those."

Paraphrasing comments such as these doesn't literally tax your vocabulary, but still it takes some imagination. It involves an uncommon mental exercise; we are rarely asked to think this way. We respond to others reflexively in day-to-day conversation, but we need to do it reflectively in VTS. Unless we listen well, we can throw ourselves off by thinking we know what a child is going to say. We really want to think about, "What did I just hear? What's the message? How can I put that into my own words?"

Here's the gist of the task: we are asked to find ways to make sure that everyone, including the child who spoke, understands an idea that was maybe not all that clearly expressed in the first place. Or is very short. Or seemingly out of nowhere. We turn the nugget provided into shared communication.

For most of us, getting really good at paraphrasing takes time, and the way we improve is to keep doing it and then stepping back to think, "Was that the best way I could have said that? Can I see from the child's expression if I got it? Is the conversation moved along in a good way because of what I said?"

A side effect of this effort is how conscious we become of our own expression and of others around us. We think about the qualities of language we use to communicate everyday. Learning to paraphrase well gives us a way to grow. Importantly, we don't let our limitations or lack of imagination limit kids' potential.

ADVICE FROM TEACHERS

Let's return to the teachers whose reflections we read at the beginning of this chapter. How did they learn to use VTS?

Anna Miller's early childhood centers in Detroit had the advantage of involving the entire staff in the training from the beginning. From the start, teachers could talk to one another, explore challenges together, and assess changes in themselves and their students as they went along. They had first encountered VTS with the guidance of Dori Jacobsohn, and Dori continued to visit over the three years they were officially implementing.

When she visited, Dori watched as teachers taught, coached, and conducted debriefings. These meetings provided opportunities for teachers to discuss as a group what they were experiencing—what they noticed happening with students and themselves. The debriefings were built around sharing stories and probing what elements of

VTS provoked the responses witnessed. If even the quietest children begin to participate, for example, what is it about VTS that makes that happen? Or why the phrasing of the questions? Why no follow-up questions?

In chapter 2, I provided answers to these questions and others. Let's see how well explanations have stuck. Test yourself. What do you remember? Write down all you can remember about why quiet kids participate. What are the basic questions? What learning is each intended to initiate? Why are there no follow-up questions? Why do we ask you to maintain an even, neutral demeanor? If you can't recall what I said, you can always refer back; consider this an open book test. Chapter 2 goes into detail about VTS elements. But even better, give yourself time to think about each question and construct your own answers based on past experience and knowledge.

Of course, Dori did some explaining for the teachers in Detroit, as I have in this book. However, in the same way children figure out what's going on in an image without input from the teacher, the principle in a discussion-based approach to training is that using your head and experience to come to understand VTS is a surer way to learn.

Understanding of images emerges from discussions; it's never all there is to know about the image, but it's a satisfying and appropriate way to start a process that leads to knowing. Understanding the pedagogy involved in VTS is best aided by your making notes about what you see during discussions and figuring out for yourself answers to your questions. Your answers also won't be all there is to know or say, but they move you forward in the process more surely than reading or hearing explanations.

The prevailing theory is that people learn by watching, hearing, memorizing, and repeatedly practicing. I'm sure you already know that I don't think those processes are enough to guarantee the kind of learning that gets internalized and sticks. I'm awfully glad that medical education doesn't stop with lectures and book learning. While talking has a minimal role as a way to learn in school today, it is the principle behind a lot of learning outside of school—talking with therapists to try to understand emotional issues, for example, or sharing ideas with a creative team in all sorts of business, research, and medical collaborations. To put it very simply, if we want to learn French, we sooner or later have to start talking.

You can make the matter of learning VTS both easier and more fun if you find others to partner with you. You might build interest by way of a small reading group around this book. Even better, find at least one other teacher to try VTS in the classroom and create a schedule of lessons you follow together. You then have a built-in resource to consult when you want to noodle through answers to questions like those above or ones that come up for you as you practice.

Sarah O'Leary echoes that and adds a thought that, oddly enough, might make it easier to get started: "Play by rules before you break them."[8] Free yourself to dive in by memorizing the questions. When it's clear to you what to ask when, you know what to do as you move from one comment to the next. You don't have to think about your next step and instead can concentrate on the children—listening well, pointing accurately, and paraphrasing.

Sarah continues, "The best way to see how it works is to try it as recommended. A certain kind of magic happens if you follow the rules—like sticking to a recipe when you're baking. Doubts peal away when you watch children respond."[9] Once you've got the basics, you can tweak the recipe to address the particulars of your students.

More advice from Meg Brown: "Don't be afraid. It's worth it simply to dive in. Just remember that it takes time to sink in. I've been doing it for two years and I'm still learning to do it effectively."[10]

Here's some advice from me: Be kind to yourself. Rigid adherence to the method is never the point; perfect VTS is not the goal. Doing VTS the best you can so that you help your students most: that's the idea. Let the children see you as their learning support in this way.

MUSEUM VISITS: A COMPANION TO
CLASSROOM DISCUSSIONS

When asked what stood out for them as particularly helpful in their training, several Detroit teachers mentioned trips to their local museum, the Detroit Institute of Arts. The DIA is within walking distance of Wayne State University and the learning centers' classrooms. The museum arranged to have the children visit on days the museum was closed to others. The classes had the luxury of galleries to themselves. Teachers also had some of their training experiences at the museum, and this is what one teacher said:

> *I enjoyed the field trips to the DIA. Having the museum closed allowed children to focus on images and listen to each other more carefully with fewer distractions. I also enjoyed the teacher discussions and participating in VTS at an adult level . . . I found the debriefings after VTS reflective and helpful for bettering myself in the VTS process.*[11]

The administrative director of one of the centers wrote, "Field trips were helpful for me as an observer and to test out a 'what would I have said' approach. Confirmations and other perspectives were gathered through debriefings."[12] The chance to watch others teach and pull back to reflect on it is not just a benefit for administrators. Teachers talking about teaching is usually very productive talk, and generally too little time is allotted to it. This work is often easier to accomplish when taken out of the school context—a mini retreat.

Others echoed the benefit of a new environment for the children too. Not every museum is as accommodating as the Detroit Institute of Arts, but many will try to make it easy for little ones to explore and for teachers to lead them in discussions. Many museums have staff trained in VTS to help if that seems useful. Many have studios too and a chance for children to make as well as look. In any case, taking children to a museum or gallery is an additional exposure that broadens the whole experience.

TAPES USED TO HELP REFLECT

Our friend Dori Jacobsohn argues for the use of making tapes to help people learning VTS. I first introduced this topic in this book by way of discussions that took place in the classroom of Sarah O'Leary. Sarah constantly uses her telephone to make tapes that she uses in her ongoing reflective practice and to share with others, like me. Sarah wrote:

> *Learning VTS is greatly aided by making videotapes. Not only do teachers get to see and learn from watching themselves but also they have a way of studying children—groups and individuals—and a tool for sharing classroom activity with parents. VTS is sometimes hard to explain: a tape does the trick.*[13]

Taping is simple these days when it's for the purposes of self-study or similar limited uses. You might not put your tapes on YouTube, but when you want a chance to reflect on what happens during your VTS— or any lessons—you can set up a smart phone in such a way that it takes in both you and at least a swath of your students. (If kids notice you doing it, they'll forget about it quickly.)

Lise White teaches two- and three-year-olds at Charlestown Nursery School. She attests to the usefulness of videotaping classes:

> *Stephanie [her partner teacher] and I laughed as we looked at a tape made two years ago when we started trying VTS. We set up a circle of chairs and tried to make a game of sitting. It became an activity of its own, something we didn't expect or want. We were put to work policing. We put an end to that and have a much looser arrangement for the children now, and at least one child is being held at any given point, for their comfort, not for our control. It's not a good idea to expect kids not to move, so we are pretty loose about it now and actually have their attention for decent discussions.*
>
> *One thing we've come to be pretty flexible about is them getting up to point to what they don't have language for. We ask for words first, of course, in part to avoid a "monkey see, monkey do" chain reaction. But another*

way it helps is that it allows them to be the little kids they are—a little bit of empowerment—not to mention that it resolves the "need to wiggle" factor, making it easier for them to sit while others talk. I really pinpoint what they are talking about when pointing so they know I'm listening to them and get used to it. If they aren't allowed to get up and show us what they notice, we risk inferring too much from the little they say. And if you misunderstand, you somewhat defeat the purpose: VTS is very much about being heard and understood. If you think you do but you don't, what does that teach?[14]

Of course, that litany of insights didn't come solely from looking at tapes. Still, when you're conducting VTS discussions, the need to be 100 percent present and to maintain a reasonable pace precludes the possibility of your remembering all you'd like to. You can't really stop and say, "What just happened?" Here's a list of some of the items you can look for as you review a tape:

- if you got the wording of the questions right
- if your paraphrasing is as accurate and helpful as you want it to be
- if your pacing gives each child her or his due but keeps things moving
- if you missed hands that were out of your direct line of vision
- if you missed chances to link related ideas

Don't just watch what you do. Examine the children's behavior too. You can stop a tape to think about what you just saw or replay a section to get a sense of what's going on with each child in a way that's hard to do as you facilitate. Given a second chance by way of tape, you can think about exactly these issues:

- who's participating and who isn't
- what kinds of comments you hear (one word or more detailed, for example)

- who repeats what someone else has said
- who seems to listen to others
- how a child's ways of participating change over time
- who might be ready for the second question

By way of tape, you can monitor all sorts of behaviors that tell you what's happening and what to improve on or what to work on next.

Tapes of classes are particularly useful when you are trying to learn VTS on your own. Many people have; Jacqueline Chung in Singapore is an example. Ideally, everyone learning would have a coach. Data regarding professional development says coaching is the single surest way to learn something new and monitor progress. With the help of tape, however, you can effectively coach yourself. You can see how you are doing and, more importantly, see how the students respond.

If you have found a partner teacher or two and set a schedule so that you conduct discussions in tandem, you can use tapes to help you compare notes. Ideally, you'd also get a chance to watch each other teach. While it's always great to see how someone else handles things, it's an even bigger benefit for you to sit back and watch your kids at work in a way you cannot do when you're teaching. Reflecting with a partner can be the start of a community of practice focused on teaching and learning.

A SCHOOL TAKES ON VTS

I want to close this chapter with a few words about Charlestown Nursery School whose teachers have contributed so much to this book. The school was founded in 2007 by Kelly Pellagrini, Kristin Valdamanis, Karen Tompros, and a core group of parents. Now Cady Audette and Kelly Pellagrini codirect the school of almost one hundred students attending a range of programs designed to fit the needs of different ages, from two-year-old toddlers to five-year-olds soon bound for kindergarten. I'm not the only one who has studied it as a model: over five hundred people from around the globe have visited to see CNS's innovative approaches to pedagogy and organization. You've been reading the words of CNS teachers throughout this book.[15]

One of the most enlightened decisions the board and leadership made as they started was to pay well for the single most important element in the teaching/learning equation: great teachers and great teaching. While they have a wonderful, well-equipped, and attractive space, the major part of their budget goes to excellent faculty salaries. To ensure that the teaching is the best that it can be, the school policy is to allot an hour to keeping up with research and trends in progressive early learning for every hour teachers spend with children. They undertake changes in teaching only after findings have been fully examined and discussed by everybody who might be affected by a change. They explored VTS using this thoughtful, thorough approach. CNS is an available model of the benefits of a community of practice.

Kelly and Cady first heard about VTS in various trainings they attended and by way of Cady's work in museums. They were reintroduced by a parent, Dabney Hailey, a long-time VTS practitioner mostly working in the context of museums and higher education. Dabney enrolled her three-year-old son at CNS for two years before he headed off to kindergarten, and she shared her enthusiasm for VTS with Kelly and Cady, seeing a fit between it and the school's approach to learning.

It's hardly rare for parents to have a great discovery they want to share with their kids' teachers, so Kelly and Cady politely thanked Dabney for the suggestion and said they'd look into it. True to their word, they did the research, reading and watching what they could online, attending a workshop at the Eric Carle Museum of Picture Book Art, and mulling it over between them even before they shared VTS with teachers.

They finally decided to mention what they had learned at a faculty meeting, and somewhat to their surprise, teachers were enthusiastic and wanted to know more. They contacted Dabney and asked her to do a demonstration. After the teachers had an image discussion among themselves, they were further intrigued, and shortly afterward, Dabney was asked to do a half-day training. Teachers were then invited to try the technique with their students on a voluntary basis working within the usual teams. Their insights have punctuated and animated this book. As you can tell, VTS is deeply woven into the fabric of the school.

Kelly and Cady generously gave me access to teachers, letting me conduct lengthy interviews and follow-up communications by e-mail. They let me watch as many classes as I could; they also let me teach myself. They also shared many insights gained over the roughly five-year history of VTS at CNS. Given their continuous presence in the school, these two remarkably engaged and supportive administrators see not only formal teaching but also informal interactions between students and teachers. They've noticed children ask each other for evidence when they read stories. They cite the influence of VTS on what they call "civil discourse" in the school: the way that children talk to each other, to teachers, and to their parents. It has become one of the "languages of learning" shared by teachers, supplementary to the Reggio Emilia Approach that is the most basic and prominent of these.

Since CNS kids don't come home with worksheets, the school needs ways to make the teaching and learning coherent and visible to parents. When parents are new to the school and therefore to VTS, they receive cards with images on one side and the VTS questions on the other. CNS teachers encourage parents to use the questions as a way to reconsider quizzing their kids and to do more to spur dialogue at home as well as school.

When parents make this effort, Kelly and Cady feel parents are better informed about their children's abilities and knowledge than when they ask litanies of questions to which there are specific answers: "What's that?" Or "What color is this?" Or "How many do you see?" When parents instead ask, "What do you notice?" they get an answer that's usually more interesting than anticipated, and they stand to learn much more besides: they hear how a child makes meaning and connections. Through this process, parents also gain insight into the pedagogical principles of CNS.

Because the questions have become second nature for many of the teachers, Kelly and Cady see them in use as teacher teams prepare end-of-day notes: "What happened with the children today?" When they write parents, they are able to say, "We noticed . . ." Or "We heard your child say . . ." "We think this because . . ."

MOVING ALONG

I hope this book gives you a sense of what teachers have learned about VTS while implementing it. I also hope the suggestions built into many of their comments help you as you start trying it out yourself. There is one more piece I want to build into this exploration of VTS before you do, though.

In chapter 6, I focus on how VTS nests within various well-established theoretical frameworks—ones that argue for child-centered teaching and learning. Having addressed the foundational theory that backs up the kind of pedagogy VTS represents, I describe existing models of student-driven approaches, ones with which VTS fits symbiotically, Montessori and Reggio Emilia schools.

AT A GLANCE: SELF-STUDY OF VTS

Learning VTS is a matter of practicing it and reflecting on what happens as a result. This learning is one small part memorizing (committing the questions to memory, for example; it's not very hard and it's very freeing), one part simply doing it, and one part thinking about what you see happening with your students as result. As I promised, I've included a set of questions to prompt the reflection half of the "practice and reflect" equation.

To summarize the process:

- To start your practice, find an image you think will work with your students, using the illustrations in this book as guides to selecting pictures. Of course, you can download any of these images from the Internet to start teaching.
- Use one image for each discussion and plan on between ten and fifteen minutes.
- Examine the picture you've chosen to make it easier to find observations and follow comments.
- Memorize the questions outlined in the section "At a Glance: VTS for Preschool" at the end of chapter 2.
- Review the sample discussions and explanations in chapters 1 and 2 to make sure you're clear about the other facilitation elements.
- Make sure you're focused and ready to listen. At first, simply make sure you're paraphrasing each comment. You can add in conditional language and linking later.

Once you've made the first step—practicing VTS with your students—give yourself some time to reflect on what happened. Continue to do this after each lesson. Reflecting is more than helpful if you want your practice to become the best it can be.

The following questions are designed to help with the last part—your reflection process. Create some kind of journal or log in which to write your answers. Don't try to answer all the questions at once; take on a few at a time. Each one has multiple answers, and what you think when you start might change in time, or at least become more nuanced. Save your answers for future reference and keep adding to them as you gain experience and new insights. Start each answer with at least two ideas.

- Why are images good topics for discussion by small children?
- Why is VTS done with a group?

- What purposes are served by having a modest age range within a group?
- What are the elements of a "good question" for preschool-age children?
- What learning is sought by each of the VTS questions?
- What are effective ways to teach listening?
- What purposes are served by pinpointing student observations?
- What purposes are served by paraphrasing?
- What is added to paraphrasing when you use conditional language?
- In what ways might VTS serve as a useful adjunct to other means of teaching language?
- What purposes are served by treating all students identically?
- What are the criteria for a lesson to be developmentally appropriate?
- What criteria define student-centered teaching?
- What does it mean to teach through inquiry?
- How does VTS support your values as a teacher? What's in it for you?
- What new does VTS bring to your overall curriculum?
- How does it help you meet the needs and potential of your students?
- How would you describe the strengths of VTS?
- What do you see as its limitations?

CHAPTER 6

Dedicated to Wonder

Keeping Preschool Child Centered

LONG AGO, WHEN MY children were little, I noticed that when I took the time to stand back and watch as they explored on their own, I would inevitably experience random flashes of joy. Kids seem to know or at least feel something that many of us grown-ups have forgotten: the pleasure of simply being alive.

I'm sure that awareness needs no explaining to the readers of this book. It's likely one of the reasons you choose to spend your days with little ones, and it certainly explains my pleasure visiting preschools, something I've done a lot in recent years. Kid-inspired delight.

I believe it's the responsibility of preschools to keep that delight alive. I asked Dori Jacobsohn for her take on what she observed and learned from the three years of working at the Detroit learning centers:

Part of the beauty of seeing VTS used in preK is that over the time it takes teachers to absorb the practice, they find more things to talk about with children and reasons to use interesting vocabulary with their kids. It also seems to support the discovery for children of how interesting it is to listen to others. It supports reflective practice and encourages being child-centered all of the time.[1]

We've not really addressed "child-centered" teaching in so many words up to this point. VTS is an example of it: the teacher is not the authority or the source of knowledge but is a facilitator of process. All decisions about what to see, think about, and comment on are up to the students. The teaching structure allows children freedom of thought and expression. Teachers step into a supportive role.

What Carly Reagan mentioned—a certain low-level frustration returning to right-wrong lessons in the wake of VTS—speaks to this issue: the practice encourages being child-centered all the time.

In this chapter, we deal more thoroughly with the theoretical underpinnings of student-driven, developmentally based teaching and learning. We also delve more deeply into why VTS assists with language development, alongside the other means you have for teaching children to express themselves verbally. We explore how VTS fits within a framework designed to prepare children for a future not wholly predicted as yet but in which they need to become active participants. And I argue that VTS helps build skills in preschool that will continue to serve them well through school and outside of it.

I include all this information partly to satisfy whatever curiosity you have about why VTS is the way it is. But in truth, my real reason is that I want to change how we think about school. Rarely is teaching and learning fun for children after preschool and maybe kindergarten. Plus, preschool fun is in jeopardy as more and more top-down academic demands supplant time for exploration, play, and independence. To me, fun is serious.

Here's an example of a moment that was serious fun for a little one—and for me. I remember a day during a family holiday when my older grandchild—now a world-weary eleven-year-old—was three. Everyone was setting out on the twenty-minute trek down a dirt road to the beach, with Wyla and me bringing up the rear. Before we were halfway down the driveway, she stopped to pick up a particularly interesting stick. Then she noticed a patch of sand, and her inner artist emerged. The stick was a perfect thing with which to do a little drawing.

When the others stopped and called to us to get a move on, I responded saying we were kinda busy, so they should go ahead; we'd catch up at some point. Or maybe not, as it later turned out because, of course, while drawing, she noticed a caterpillar, and she moved on from art making to science, trying to coax it onto her stick. With a little nudge from me, she did capture the poor creature that, she apparently decided, would rather be on a leaf she found than on her stick after all. By the time the others were spreading their towels on the sand, I suppose, we had just made it to the road where a puddle offered new and different delights. My job, it seemed, was narrating, identifying, naming, asking and answering questions, and of course, making sure that she was never in danger.

We made it to the beach that sunny afternoon just before the others were ready to pack up, and even then it was only because Wyla had tired of exploring at some point and asked to climb into a canvas tote so that she could be carried the rest of the way.

As I lugged her toward the water, I had time to realize that to her the destination mattered only a little bit. The beach was just another place to dig and maybe gingerly approach the untrustworthy surf. It was the journey that mattered. It's impossible to quantify what she learned during our journey, but learn she did; I'm sure of it—and it was entirely fun.

Preschool ought to be a constant journey, or so it seems to me. The job of teachers is similar to that of grandparents, at least as I perceive the role of both. We open doors and keep the path safe. We narrate the discoveries. We answer questions and ask just as many. We direct our children's gazes to wonderful things they might otherwise miss but more often we get to enjoy what they find. We let some things remain mysterious. We help them chart their own course, not only ours, offering options but mostly trying to help them explore. Through exploring, they find themselves as much as they discover the world.

Of course, we adults have to help them become socialized human beings, too, learning how to be family members, friends, collaborators, and eventually students. But this endeavor works so much better if we demonstrate manners rather than teaching children the rules. We play with them and help them figure out how to share and play with others. We take them places and introduce a variety of stimulating resources. We let them help us with appropriate real-life tasks—authentic work, not make-work. We demonstrate communication; we listen and give them language they need to express their thoughts and engage with others as we converse. We read to them and point to words as we introduce them to the marvels of stories told in writing and pictures. We let them draw and paint as much as they wish and allow them to make their own decisions whenever it makes sense. We encourage their "whys" and delight in their wonder.

You get the picture. We don't waste these years of wonder. Knowing how fertile their minds and imaginations are during these early years, we help children use these to form a strong foundation on which later experience rests. We make them confident about the validity of their curiosity, interests, and their own ability to learn. In this chapter, I focus on teaching programs dedicated to wonder—and how VTS helps nurture both rigor and delight.

THE CHALLENGES OF PRESSURE FOR ACADEMICS IN PRESCHOOL

We have more than enough evidence of what happens if we don't support children's wonder and ability to learn on their own. Before they reach first grade, many children have lost the excitement at learning we see as they move from infancy toward school: the eagerness to try everything, the curiosity that seems innate, the expressiveness that simply flows. This remarkable energy dissipates unless we nurture it and keep it alive—and it seems that, collectively at least, we don't.

Erika Christakis, author of *The Importance of Being Little: What Preschoolers Really Need from Grownups*, wrote about this phenomenon *in* the *Atlantic* in early 2016. She titled her article "The New Preschool Is Crushing Kids."

Preschool classrooms have become increasingly fraught spaces, with teachers cajoling their charges to finish their "work" before they can go play. And yet, even as preschoolers are learning more pre-academic skills at earlier ages, I've heard many teachers say that they seem somehow—is it possible?—less inquisitive and less engaged than the kids of earlier generations. More children today seem to lack the language skills needed to retell a simple story or to use basic connecting words and prepositions. They can't make a conceptual analogy between, say, the veins on a leaf and the veins in their own hands.

New research sounds a particularly disquieting note. A major evaluation of Tennessee's publicly funded preschool system, published in September [2015], found that although children who had attended preschool initially exhibited more "school readiness" skills when they entered kindergarten than did their non-preschool-attending peers, by the time they were in first grade their attitudes toward school were deteriorating. And by second grade they performed worse *on tests measuring literacy, language, and math skills. The researchers told* New York *magazine that overreliance on direct instruction and repetitive, poorly structured pedagogy were likely culprits; children who'd been subjected to the same insipid tasks year after year after year were understandably losing their enthusiasm for learning.*

That's right. The same educational policies that are pushing academic goals down to ever earlier levels seem to be contributing to—while at the same time obscuring—the fact that young children are gaining fewer *skills, not more.*[2]

Christakis is hardly alone caring and writing about this phenomenon. Coming at it from a slightly broader standpoint, Nancy Carlsson-Paige offers an extensive critique, not just of schools, but of the whole commercial enterprise that has grown up during the past thirty years around media and related products, heavily marketed to very young children and their families. Both the passivity of the child's role in most of them and the replacement of imaginative play with prescriptive toys have negative implications for natural development. In her very read-able book *Taking Back Childhood*, Carlsson-Paige chronicles multiple stories decrying missing elements in a constructive childhood:

> *Unfortunately if parents . . . turn to the school system to foster the type of imaginative play that is being stamped out by so many of the media and products marketed to children today, they may be sorely disappointed. As a professor of early childhood education who has spent twenty-five years helping dedicated people learn how to teach and encourage children, I am truly shocked by what is happening to primary education in America today. The federal government now mandates that all ninety-one thousand public schools in the United States be rated on the basis of their students' stan-dardized test scores.*
>
> *My friend Roz stopped by my house the day she decided to stop teach-ing kindergarten in the Boston public schools after more than thirty years. As she burst through my front door, Roz said, "I quit today. I can't stand to see what's happening to kids. Kindergarten is nothing like it used to be. The blocks, water table, science corner with birds nests and feathers are all gone—there's no time. It's all learn the alphabet and reading and writing.*[3]

Neither kindergarten nor preschool teachers are at fault for this situation. Curriculum mandates and academic directives come from above. The pressure from publishers and commercial purveyors of materials on both schools and families is intense in part because of ubiquitous marketing. Parents who likely don't recall their own early schooling have been made to believe that success today is dependent on the early acquisition of skills in reading, writing, and math. Meanwhile, children see parents deeply engaged in media throughout the day, and few would rather build with a set of blocks or draw than do what they see grownups doing.

There is no single culprit for the "loss of childhood," and neither is there a simple solution; it's a complex web of commercialism, policy, and achievement criteria generated by many sources. There is no single place to lay the blame and no easy way to change the situation. Still, fixes are hiding in plain sight.

In my view, the "fraught spaces" described by Christakis, Carlsson-Paige, and others are operating based on wrong-headed goals and objectives, and it doesn't stop at preschool. If we address preschool, as Christakis does, more and more data suggest that the push toward a narrow definition of "school readiness"—knowing letters, numbers, and the like—is counterproductive. A more logical system would respond to this data by abandoning efforts that aren't working and return to something that is more developmentally appropriate, more useful for children as a foundation, and a whole lot more engaging.

ARGUMENTS FOR CHILD-CENTERED LEARNING

John Dewey

The wisdom backing a different course than we are currently on is more than a century old. Writing in 1897, John Dewey (1859–1952) encapsulated what became known as progressive education in his "Pedagogic Creed." "I believe that education . . . is a process of living and not a preparation for future living" is one point included in a long list of beliefs regarding what school is.[4] Make schooling a part of the activity of living that goes on all around us, he says, not a separate arena reserved for academic challenge. Fold teaching and learning into the full dimensions of cognition rather than confining it to achieve a narrow set of skills and limited body of knowledge.

Regarding the subject matter of education, Dewey states, "It is true that language is a logical instrument, but it is fundamentally and primarily a social instrument."[5] We learn language to communicate with one another, and yes, to use it as a tool to define, delineate, and inform. It's a tool of both intellect and emotions, however, and we shouldn't teach it as words and grammar or to pass tests, but to be integral parts of a community of fully expressive human beings.

Regarding the nature of method, Dewey writes, "I believe that the image is the great instrument of instruction. What a child gets out of any subject presented to him is simply the images [that] he himself forms with regard to it."[6] As I have argued, our eyes are immensely useful tools from infancy on. We learn by using them and images are a "great instrument of instruction." Clearly, that understanding is a principal argument for the immediate appeal and the impact of VTS, but it's more than that. Images are at the core of understanding what we read, of science, of history, of applied math. And so on.

Dewey had early experience teaching, first high school and then elementary, but he was more interested in observing and writing about learning than in practicing it. He was an astute and active observer—creating a lab school at the University of Chicago, where he was on the faculty of the philosophy department—and wrote at length arguing his ideas from the standpoint of psychology as much as any narrow view of pedagogy.

Over the course of many decades, Dewey elaborated an entire philosophy of education that elucidates and elaborates the creed's bullet points. I cherry-picked among a long list of them and did so because of how these nuggets relate to VTS and to my wishes for preschool based on authentic experience, not academic exercises. Nonetheless, Dewey's big ideas come across based on virtually any selection of tenets.

In keeping with his view of education as "a process of living," Dewey believed in what we now call "hands on," or learning by doing. Learning involves action; it is never passive. Although he firmly believed that the teacher has a critical role, it was not as the dispenser of information or assigner of tasks, but as responsible for creating a rigorous environment for learning—and it's within such a structure that children construct understanding of what they need to know and be able to do.

Because to some extent Dewey can be credited with the notion of child-centered education, at some point during the trajectory of his involvement as an observer of educational process, he became concerned that many practitioners were misreading the concept. Child centering looked to him to be a license for the lack of discipline, never his intent. Critics of Dewey have always been disappointed, however, that he wasn't able to create a working model that demonstrated methodologies based on the precepts of his psychologically and philosophically grounded theory. That missing model probably explains why he's not had more or at least more consistent impact on the creation of methods and spaces in which children learn more important basic skills than memorizing numbers and letters. He's always been a beacon for me because he believed both in child agency and in structure. He is partial inspiration for VTS because of his support for learning language within a social environment—discussion is an example—and for key insights into the role imagery plays in effecting learning.

Jean Piaget

Jean Piaget (1896–1980) is another source for recognizing what's wrong-headed about the current academic thrusts in preschool. Like others who have contributed to what we know about early childhood learning, Piaget was also an empirical scientist—one who learned from the accumulation of observations to try to understand something as objectively as possible. Trained in psychology, Piaget developed strategies to enable him to come up with data from which educators could and can generalize. As much as possible, he watched to see what his subjects did naturally, and he kept copious notes about what he saw, beginning with infants and watching as they changed over time. He also assigned tasks and interventions to study the responses.

Piaget contributed several essential elements to inspire and guide child-centered learning. The best known is his stage theory of development: he concluded that what happens cognitively can be seen through behavior patterns that dominate for periods in time, roughly corresponding to ages. These patterns—stages—can be described in detail and are essentially inevitable, predictable, and unavoidable; they are dictated not only by evolving capabilities within the brain and body but also by interactions with the social environment—with people, things, and phenomena around us. What humans learn, what we come to know, what we are able to do is socially constructed, he argued; growth and change don't simply happen but develop in response to what we encounter in our physical and social environments.

Although subsequent scholars have built on, expanded, and refined the groundbreaking insights of Piaget in the almost one hundred years since he first published *The Language and Thought of the Child* in 1926, most effective teaching, especially during the critical early years that include preschool, owes a significant debt to him. In case you need to brush up on your Piaget, I recommend *A Piaget Primer: How a Child Thinks* by Dorothy G. Singer and Tracey A. Revenson. Here is how they summarize Piaget's "Preoperational Stage: Ages Two Through Seven," ages that cover preschool:

> *The child in the preoperational stage is not yet able to think logically. With the acquisition of language, the child is able to represent the world through mental images and symbols, but in this state, these symbols depend on his own perception and his intuition. The preoperational child is completely egocentric. Although he is beginning to take a greater interest in the objects and people around him, he sees them from only one point of view: his own. This stage could be labeled the "age of curiosity": preschoolers are always questioning and investigating new things. Since they know the world only from their limited experience, they make up explanations when they don't have one. Children's beliefs that natural phenomena are man-made and that everything has life are ways in which they create explanation for confusing experiences.*
>
> *It is during the preoperational stage that children's thought differs most from adults.*[7]

Paying attention to the strengths and limitations of preoperational cognition allows teaching to be organized to help the child behave naturally but still grow. The paradigm shifts from "learn this because you're going to need it later" to "let me help you reach your potential now." Since my subject here is VTS, let me point to the ways in which I see VTS respecting Piaget's preoperational stage boundaries, playing to existing strengths and trying to push the child along to behaviors within reach:

- VTS focuses on preschoolers' curiosity and willingness to explore; children are given permission to wonder and support for doing so along with others. Attention is directed, but thinking is not.
- Imagery and language are intertwined at preschool ages, explaining in part the constant presence of illustrations in books as well as why children easily respond to requests to look and talk about what they see in images, a central precept of VTS.
- While artists create images with intentions and logic, VTS allows for children to understand these images based on their own logic (or illogic), not the artist's or the teacher's. Whatever logic is applied is theirs. That said, the second question, asking for evidence, nudges them toward evidence-based logic, a cognitive capability within reach.
- Images for preschool VTS are chosen to let children use what they know to figure out meaning. They explain what they find in their own terms, and as Piaget predicts, they are usually egocentric. Over the course of a discussion, VTS allows a variety of egocentric views to rest comfortably side by side, and the notion that "my view isn't the only possibility" is nurtured naturally and sympathetically.
- Given the predictability of idiosyncrasy, teachers have a wonderful glimpse into how children think and feel and often into their concerns. Different from adults as children are, one constant VTS delight is the way comments surprise us, as so many teachers have said.

Kelly Pellagrini and Cady Audette, codirectors of the Charlestown Nursery School, believe that if parents can be enticed to use VTS questions instead of more directive ones, they too have a rare chance to know and appreciate not just what their children know, but who they are.

Lev Vygotsky, Abigail Housen, and Maria Montessori

The "behaviors within reach" mentioned previously is a concept introduced earlier in this book in conjunction with Lev Vygotsky (1896–1934) and his well-substantiated theory that at any given moment, children operate within a zone of actual and potential ability that he called the "zone of proximal behavior."[8]

Let's say that, as of now, a child knows this and can do that. With some sort of slight assist (his reference is to help from a "more capable peer"), that child can also do something more, but the more will be what's within reach, what the child is on the verge of knowing or being able to do, what's "proximal."

As we constructed VTS using Abigail Housen's data on aesthetic thought (how people think when looking at art), we knew both what beginning viewers—preschool children, for example—could do (for example, make observations) and what ability was within reach (drawing inferences from observations). We created questions to function as part of the appropriate assist and put children together in groups so that their different observations could help all observe more. Those children who were slightly ahead of the curve in terms of making inferences would provide assistance by example.[9]

Operating at the same time as Dewey and Piaget but with the intent to produce actual teaching models, not just theory, Maria Montessori (1870–1952) was a particularly influential proponent of child-centered teaching. As a scientist, educator, medical doctor, and pediatric specialist, she developed an early commitment to education, initially in the service of children with disabilities and learning challenges. Having become known for that work and for her ever-expanding knowledge of educational practice and history, she was asked to open a school in 1907 for the children of working parents in an apartment building established for low-income families in Rome. She didn't teach at the school but put her training as a scientist to work observing what happened when another did.

Montessori came to see that the conventional methods of the time confined what she saw as natural development, limiting a child's capabilities instead of broadening them. To see what happened if she created an alternative set of options, she started experimenting with both the setup of the classrooms and the methods of teaching, something she continued doing throughout her life.

Her innovations included creating the kinds of environments that we find in preschools everywhere today. For example, she redesigned furniture to make it child sized, freeing children to move around easily so that, instead of being regimented, they were allowed choice among activities. She paid close attention to what children gravitated toward when not directed and what captured and held their attention. Among her discoveries were how much children preferred engaging in activities they saw happen in real life, how they thrived with a certain amount of independence, and how when given activities they appreciated, they developed what she called "spontaneous self-discipline."

As she gathered data, she solidified a method described in her 1917 book, *Spontaneous Activity in Education*. In it, she says something that particularly resonates with me:

> To observe it is necessary to be "trained" and this is the true way of approach to science. For if phenomena cannot be seen, it is if they did not exist, while, on the other hand, the soul of the scientist is entirely possessed by a passionate interest in what he sees. He who has been "trained" to see begins to feel interest, and such interest is the motive-power [that] creates the spirit of the scientist.[10]

The way she wrote is old fashioned, but the way I read it is that the child's "passionate interest" in so many things is undisciplined, and for it to become a useful tool in science, it must be focused and honed.

(I would add that's true for other disciplines as well; curiosity is not all you need to be a historian or mathematician.) Observing is the essential tool of science, however: if phenomena remain unseen, it's as if they didn't exist. Scientists are obsessed with seeing and inherently fascinated by what they see. Seeing "creates the spirit of the scientist." I would argue that that spirit is very much alive in young children; they are born with the "spirit of the scientist."

It's probably not difficult to fathom why Montessori's statement appeals to me. VTS supplies "training" in directing the eye and finding meaning, and of course, the second question provides another essential ingredient for science and other disciplines, backing up ideas with visual evidence. But VTS trains the eye and the mind in the service of child-directed exploration. While VTS begins with stories told in images, the skills learned quickly transfer to observing, say, creatures in an aquarium or picture books of animals.

Jacqueline (Jackie) Cossentino provided my window into VTS and Montessori philosophy and practice. Jackie became aware of VTS shortly after it was born in 1991 and eventually acted as a VTS trainer operating mostly in Massachusetts and Connecticut. Her Montessori background, according to the website of the National Center for Montessori in the Public Sector where she is Director of Research, began not long after VTS came into her life, when as a parent she carefully watched what happened in her son's preschool.[11]

Jackie currently oversees the center's development of evidence-based tools for evaluation, assessment, and continuous improvement. The center started its work in 2012 with the "twin goals of expanding access to Montessori education for all families and strengthening the quality of existing public Montessori programs."[12] Jackie frequently publishes the results of her research and equally often uses it to help schools that want to examine their practice with a focus on improvement.

Jackie and her colleagues operate within several overlapping spheres, one of which involves guiding the development of several Montessori and Montessori-inspired schools. She has built VTS into their structural plans: she believes it serves a number of foundational purposes within Montessori. In general, Montessori schools assign very little work in groups, preferring to let children direct themselves within the "prepared environments" of six learning areas. The use of images, the questions, and the supportive teacher feedback have prompted Jackie to recommend VTS for the older children—four-and-a-half- to five-year-olds (the younger ones watch)—once a week in place of "read-aloud circles." Some teachers conduct discussions more often, and all keep the images displayed after discussions in the language learning centers. Kids can and do continue conversations on their own.

VTS also resonates with a basic Montessori practice of having patterns of tried-and-true prescriptions for teaching and learning, often a sequence of questions that can be deployed when seen to be helpful— very much like how VTS questions are used by teachers cited throughout this book. As other teachers have recommended, memorizing the VTS questions allows them to become automatic, freeing teachers from having to think "what's next?" and enabling them to focus on listening to children. The purposeful wording of the VTS questions appeals to Montessori-inspired teachers. Jackie told me:

> Keeping the first question in mind allows teachers to continuously look deeply at kids for clues about what's happening with them as individuals and as they interact. Regardless of what grabs the teacher's attention, it's "What's going on here?" not "What's wrong?"[13]

She went on to say:

> As a scientist, Montessori regarded human beings as a species with discernable needs and tendencies that could be seen in each stage of development. Being a good teacher requires being grounded in the characteristics of these stages being able to consistently employ open-ended observation and analysis, abilities that VTS fosters. The benefits of VTS for children include the practice of sharing, using language, becoming empowered, developing a

voice, and knowing that what they say has a purpose and will be respected. It's also good practice at being patient. All of these are core Montessori purposes. And so is the conviction that art is a fundamental human need.[14]

Listening and Reggio Emilia

A corollary to these benefits, of course, is learning to listen, a skill that is hard to teach unless two essential preconditions are met: having something worth hearing to listen to and having some indication of what listening means. Discussions seem a natural environment in which to teach listening, but again it depends on whether the discussion meets those two criteria.

VTS addresses these conditions first by making the subject of discussions a carefully chosen image, one about which there is much to interest those in the discussion, one where comments that come forth are also likely to be stimulating to all. Second, teachers demonstrate they listen to the children by pointing and paraphrasing; they listen and they understand.

You have heard a lot from teachers at the Charlestown Nursery School, and here we return to the voice of Lise White, who teaches the youngest children. Lise describes one of the inspirations for the "culture of listening" that has emerged as a trademark of CNS. She wrote to me:

Carlina Rinaldi, former [pedagogical supervisor] in the municipal schools of Reggio Emilia, Italy and current President of the Reggio Children Foundation, coined the phrase, "The pedagogy of listening." At CNS, listening to the ideas, questions, and observations of children, families, and colleagues is one of the most important characteristics of our teaching practice. We strive, in our curriculum, environments, and practices, to create the conditions in which children learn the life long skill of listening. Listening is a practice that requires focus, attention, a calm body, and an active, but disciplined mind. During the VTS lesson, everyone present, adults and children, practice the skills required to listen.[15]

As Lise points out, this "pedagogy of listening" helps the teachers at CNS pay constant and close attention to what children say to them and to each other. They use what they learn from children's talk in much the same way as Carla Rinaldi reports is Reggio's ongoing assessment method: teachers fold what they learn into conversations among themselves. Also under consideration at CNS will be any other new data on early childhood learning, something all the teachers continually monitor. Teachers share what they learn and jointly figure out if any new approach suggests they rethink what they are doing, as they did when VTS turned up on their radar. As Kelly Pelligrini and Cady Audette told me:

> Although we continue to learn from many sources, CNS is perhaps most inspired by the schools of Reggio Emilio in terms of how we teach and also in the ways we've set up classrooms and the school in general—how we take children out into the neighborhood, and what we use as resources like recycled materials, for example. We are very thoughtful, intentional, and strategic in our decision making and that includes thinking about why to bring kids together into groups—how will they benefit. VTS discussions provide a needed opportunity to exchange ideas; the teachers facilitate but don't take charge. Kids get only one preschool experience. Conversation and dialogue are essential pieces of it. We think both build skills that are needed in the long run.[16]

The early childhood learning centers of Reggio Emilia Italy are inspiration to many child-centered schools. One of the most powerful voices in sensitively deciding what interventions produce the most natural—therefore the most valuable—learning in small children was Loris Malaguzzi (1920–1994), a founder of what is now a widely respected approach to early childhood pedagogy. A primary school teacher and an educational psychologist and, it seems, an instinctive collaborator, Malaguzzi worked with parents to rethink early schooling in the city of Reggio Emilia and surrounding small towns after World War II.

Pulling from information and theory by developmental scholars—Piaget and Vygotsky important among them—and also grounding the approach in the culture of Italian towns, Malaguzzi oversaw the gradual building of a network of schools providing early learning support that, by the 1970s, extended from infancy to age six. Paraphrasing content on the website of the Loris Malaguzzi International Centre, Reggio schools stress, "quality education" open to an as-yet-undefined future and moving beyond the disturbing past of the war years and the Hitler-aligned regime that devastated the country.[17] Reggio schools are places that put children and their potentials at the center, and the intent is to offer many occasions of creativity to children and families. Through constant, watchful processes, teachers and methods grow and change along with children and the world. Malaguzzi, Rinaldi, and their colleagues welcomed the building of a similarly dedicated international educational community.

Several principles are at the core of the approach: mutual respect, a strong sense of community often fostered through shared activities, and much opportunity for self-guided exploration. In a book one might call Reggio's manifesto, *The Hundred Languages of Children*, many Reggio practitioners describe another essential element in the Reggio approach: the wide repertory of means available to children to express themselves.[18]

In the US preschools bemoaned by author Erika Christakis, language acquisition pushes out other means of expression. While communicating by talking is a key tool in the Reggio Emilia Approach too, drawing, painting, building, and drama are on par with words and writing as viable languages. Through their individual and collective investigations—some of them long-term projects of considerable depth—children begin with their perceptions of what is and what interests them and come to form ideas and theories about how things work. They both investigate and communicate what they think through their choosing any of "one hundred languages." While we often teach language or art or science as distinct realms, Reggio-inspired teachers facilitate diverse experiences. Children convey their work processes and findings by means of their own choosing or invention. They are allowed to be their creative full human selves, something most educational arenas place little value on.

Although he was more lecturer than writer, one often-cited quote attributed to Malaguzzi contains a lot of the philosophy that appeals to schools such as CNS. He advised teachers:

> *Stand aside for a while and leave room for learning. Observe carefully what children do, and then, if you have understood well, perhaps teaching will be different from before.*[19]

To Malaguzzi, observation was as important for children as it was for teachers: carefully observe what's around you, he might have said to a child, and if you have understood well, you will know something you did not before. Reggio-inspired school environments are set up to be interesting places to explore in themselves, and venturing out of the schools and into the surrounding neighborhoods extends the turf available to observe.

His long-time associate and successor in charge of the Reggio schools, Carlina Rinaldi, elaborates on the "pedagogy of listening" in a 2004 article titled "The Relationship Between Documentation and Assessment." In it, she argues for listening as an essential element in teaching, in understanding what's happening with children, and in life:

> *A "listening context" is created when individuals feel legitimized to represent their theories and offer their own interpretation of a particular question. We enrich our knowledge and our subjectivity by listening to others and being open to them when we learn as a group. When children are working together, each is developing her own process by learning from the processes of the others. If you believe that the others are a source of your learning, your identity and your knowledge, you have opened a very important door to the joy of being together. We are not separated by our differences but*

connected by our differences. It is because of my difference that I am useful
to you because I offer another perspective. To learn as a group means to
learn from the learning of the others. This learning from others is visible,
not only because of documentation but because there is a context of listen-
ing, in which my theories are shared with the others.[20]

Reluctant as Reggio-inspired teachers are to direct the pursuits identified by children—they use group activities as sparingly as Montessori
schools—there must be good reason to interrupt the flow of children's
self-directions and congregate them. VTS seems to serve one purposeful
group activity within a Reggio atmosphere. Reggio teachers are always
interested in what children think and in helping them use their observation skills to draw conclusions. Because VTS offers a rich opportunity
for both, various Reggio experts have been receptive to VTS.

My colleague Dori Jacobsohn has introduced VTS to teachers-in-
training at a Reggio-inspired college early childhood program as well
as in the context of ongoing professional development (she trained the
Detroit teachers in VTS). She thinks that learning VTS is a gentle way
to test student-centered learning. She wrote to me:

We all come to teaching with different ideas of what the role of the teacher
is and what the role of the child is. Participating in VTS discussions as a
facilitator and also as a participant demonstrates first hand what it means
to be open to the possibilities in the child-centered approach central to
Reggio-inspired and other developmentally based, child-centered curricu-
lums. Learning VTS facilitation supports everyone's listening—students,
potential teachers and working professionals—because it demonstrates why
you listen: you learn from each other, as Rinaldi has said. The VTS ques-
tions are particularly helpful when teachers want to delve deeper into how a
child came to a certain idea, how a child thinks and views his or her world.[21]

Anna Miller, director of the early childhood centers in Detroit,
wanted children to benefit from VTS but also thought that learning

VTS would give teachers a chance to dig into what it means to teach in a child-centered way. Some already shared such understandings, but others, as with most of us, had had neither training nor their own early experience to provide insights into how and why inquiry and facilitating were valuable methods; these teachers were more comfortable with direct instruction. In a recent conversation, Anna told me:

> *Some teachers don't have an image of a teacher or understanding of teaching as meaning a facilitator and listener. They also may not have an image of a child as a contributor to their own learning. One of the reasons I wanted to bring VTS to our centers was that I wanted the opportunity for the teachers to talk about a shift of our teaching culture toward more Reggio-inspired activities, but first I saw that we had to shift some of the teachers' way of thinking. VTS has been useful in getting there.[22]*

PLAY

If there is another area within the perfect preschool—what I'm trying to describe here—one often short-changed, it's play. Nancy Carlsson-Paige creates the rationale for returning play to its rightful place in early childhood in school and out:

> *When I begin to examine what's missing from contemporary childhood, the first thing I note is the absence of creative play. All of the great child development theorists, from Lev Vygotsky and Jean Piaget to Anna Freud and Erik Erikson, saw play as vital to children's social, emotional, and cognitive growth—and perhaps the most important tool our children have to work through new experiences, ideas, and feelings. Over the course of my career, I've witnessed hundreds of children using play as a vehicle for making sense of the confusing world around them.*
>
> *One of the most striking examples that comes to mind involves a kindergarten student I taught twenty-five years ago named Ruby. In the second half of the school year, Ruby fell ill with spinal meningitis (or "spider*

*meningitis," as she would later tell her classmates), and was out of school for
at least three weeks. Upon her return to the classroom, she headed straight
to the dramatic play corner where I set up a "hospital," put on a white coat,
and was soon leaning over Sam, one of her favorite play partners and now
her "patient." I remember Ruby listening to his heart with a stethoscope,
giving him a "shot," and directing him to eat some "medicine"—a bowl full
of plastic cubes she'd mixed up just for him. And I remember her spending
much of the next few weeks in the same play area, hovering over one willing
patient after another. Finally, very slowly, Ruby began spending more time
in other parts of the classroom much as she had before she got sick.*[23]

I'm sure you have figured this out by now, but I'm trying to build
an argument for what I see as the antidote to the "fraught spaces" described by Erika Christakis in "The New Preschool Is Crushing Kids."
Many serious scholars—and there are more than I've cited here—have
used data to argue alternatives to stressing certain limited academic
skills in preschool. Both Montessori schools and ones inspired by Reggio Emilia offer coherent alternatives.

Such schools intend to be student-centered. They grant a certain
amount of autonomy to children, allowing them to make choices about
some of what to do rather than always being instructed and tightly
scheduled. Children function within an environment replete with appropriate opportunities—an area full of books and things to look at
and read, an area with art and building materials, a science area, a dramatic play corner, and so forth. This kind of arrangement is reasonably
common in preschools, but it's the freedom allowed children to make
choices about how and where they spend their time, to work alone at
times and with others at other times, to settle their own disputes and
the like that sets student-centered schools apart.

Teachers give up a certain amount of control under such circumstances, seeing themselves as facilitators of learning rather than as central
authorities. They introduce materials, advise, answer questions, super-
vise groups as needed, make sure that everyone is safe and occupied,

and occasionally call the students together for specific purposes. They see their roles as guides or resources to expedite learning rather than as sources of information and assigners of preordained tasks.

Does such pedagogy prepare students for school readiness? To some extent the answer depends on what schools expect of children later. Our achievement landscape is dominated by tests that, according to Carlina Rinaldi, who isn't alone in this sense, tell us less than we hope:

> *We see more and more often, the risk of considering testing as a tool of assessment. In reality, testing assesses only children's knowledge of the test's content, not the true learning of children.[24]*

Although measures of more broad-based learning exist—including social and emotional growth and critical thinking development—they don't carry the weight of standardized measures like the ones that Rinaldi faults. Tests and the achievement standards they are meant to assess were originally created to assure fairness: proving all students in public schools could perform up to an acceptable level, at least in reading and math.

At the time, and to a great extent still today, discrepancies existed across the demographic spectrum. Standardization doesn't seem to have been the hoped-for panacea, however. Improvements in scores have been made but not enough to merit the continuation of teaching and testing that, like the "school-readiness" priority in preschools, isn't achieving the intended goals, however laudable. Too many children still fail to achieve at the sought-after levels.

FINAL THOUGHTS ABOUT VTS, LANGUAGE, AND NOW

Standards have been broadened in recent years to incorporate more "twenty-first-century skills," but they haven't been universally embraced, and the future of standardization is unclear. In any case, there remains little indication that all children leave elementary and secondary school prepared for college or the world of ever-changing work. Or that all children, regardless of socioeconomic circumstances, achieve on an equal footing. Fair and equal education remains elusive in the United States despite decades of concern.

One intention of the ever-growing expansion of preschools is to address the language differences with which children start school. Because the language proficiency sought is "standard English," children who come to school speaking something else are dealt with as needing remediation. In this view, their other language is a weakness, not a strength. One irony here is that, while fluency in more than one language is eventually looked on as a mark of a particularly well-educated person, it's considered something to be fixed earlier.

This terrain is especially complicated because of the many languages children speak at home. When we speak of English language learners, we usually mean children who speak Spanish, Chinese, or Arabic at home. In neighborhoods of different social groups, in rural America, and in black homes, well-developed vernacular languages allow for communicative fluency even if it isn't in the language that eventually gets tested. The melting pot notion of the United States has long assumed that we are better off if we all speak a standardized tongue, but in "real lives" at home and on the streets, in music and entertainment, a great diversity is encountered and even embraced.

The language of images transcends these cultural differences. Teachers who are officially designated as teaching English for speakers of other languages have found VTS extremely helpful because as long as teachers understand what children say, children may express themselves as best they can. Teachers then can paraphrase using the mainstream form of English, anchoring vocabulary in observations and ideas in the inferences drawn from those observations. As any language specialist will tell us, for language to develop, children need to speak as well as hear language, and VTS discussions create a unique forum for both.

Nancy Pignatelli at Public School 110 in Brooklyn has taught there long enough to see what happens when a neighborhood gentrifies.

Fewer children need language props because the new influx of students arrives with a good deal of intellectual exposure as well as social and emotional support at home. However, the mix of students is useful for all; overall children come to school knowing different things, and during discussions they have a chance to scaffold on each other's insights at the same time as they learn to get along with each other. Students with experience abroad or who are smart in the ways of the streets bring valuable insights into discussions just as those who have had the advantages of resource-rich environments have much to share. A challenge to the teacher becomes appreciating what's said by all of them.

VTS as a practice opens a window into a bigger subject: the essential usefulness of discussion itself. As you well know, VTS discussions root vocabulary in images, connecting language to what is observed, but they do more: they help develop the ability to find and tell stories. They also create a bank of mental images children can use to visualize what they hear about in stories read to them and later when they read. Discussions allow children to construct new understandings of many subjects and phenomena guided by teacher questions and greatly aided by contributions of other children.

Being able to express oneself orally with clarity is an early step in literacy more generally—the essential foundation of it—and it is a capacity that remains vitally useful throughout education and later life. That said, strategies currently employed at all levels of school for building literacy rely little on open-ended speech despite its efficacy in promoting and nurturing oral language. VTS provides an efficient, easy antidote, one that can begin in preschool where it proves to be as powerful as it has in later grades.

Although most of the data is anecdotal, a consensus has formed among VTS educators that it builds a foundation in confidence, visual literacy, and listening skills. It also nurtures the ability to create opinions, express them, and back them up in evidence. Children know how to discuss and even disagree with one another, to respond to and build on the ideas of others, to work in groups as well as alone—and this happens with only biweekly discussions during the wonderfully fertile year of preschool. When looking, thinking, and talking, structured on a few questions, become a habit (as they quickly do), children have a basis for knowing how to learn.

VTS is designed to be a companion to, not a replacement for, other forms of teaching. Clearly, sometimes it's the legitimate objective of teaching—or of particular lessons within an overall approach—to lead children to make certain specific discoveries, ones that are correct and true. Guessing how many fish swim in the aquarium misses the point of teaching why you count. What is troublesome is when preschools stress hard skills that don't result in the long-term benefits that are expected, as the kind of data that Christakis has accumulated tells us.

Here's one challenge for schools: as educators, we must maintain a helpful balance of talking to kids; letting them talk; helping them listen; stretching their exposure to what's around them; and introducing new language, information, and concepts in an environment where it's most likely to be remembered and become useful. In other words, we accomplish most when we teach in the context of children's interactions with the world around them, the adults they encounter, and with other children. Useful as rote exercises can sometimes be, authentic experience is essential to the growth of children from early childhood onward. I'm in favor of rigor; I'm just against pointless regimentation for children especially during these vulnerable yet fertile years.

A huge challenge in the test-driven environment that preschool teachers must prepare their students for is being and remaining child centered. VTS can help. By stimulating children with images, interacting responsively as they share ideas, and nurturing them through positive reinforcement of effort and good facilitation, teachers can teach both speech and listening in authentic ways, using the group and the process to help individuals grow.

As often happens toward late afternoon these days, my three-and-a-half-year-old granddaughter Evhe Simone commandeered her mom's phone last evening as they were on their way to the library, and she called me on FaceTime. I love it, of course; today's tech has added much fun to being a grandparent, especially if you live at some distance. In the relatively few minutes she relegated to our conversation, I heard her ask her mom, "Why are those cars stopped?" And then, "What is that blue car doing?" And quickly thereafter, "Why are those balloons there?" As I've argued before in another context, I don't think the point of the questions is entirely to get answers, though she seemed to expect some—and her mom was quick to supply ideas. I think she's actually exhibiting her capacity for curiosity. She's trying to figure out the world and how it works, so she asks about it. She needs to think there are answers, but it's not the answers that matter; she wants to know that it's okay to wonder. To not know and to ask. It's an essential effort and every child does it.

VTS allows you to harness this glorious capacity of childhood and provide children a way to wonder with others. To freely observe and share the perceptions that come of it. To talk and listen, not just to grownups but also to others like and different from themselves. To be in their child's world and to be understood and valued for it.

Their pleasures at discovering make it clear why we teach: helping kids to be their full selves, not just what we want them to be. Through communicating with each other, they build a sense of community. They let their evolving ability to think in new ways drive their language forward. They bring the way they learn outside of school into the classroom and give rigor and legitimacy to what they've been doing since they opened their eyes as infants. They explore not just what there is to know but also how to learn.

VTS helps teachers honor and increase the incredible capacities of the early years. I hope you enjoy your adventure putting it to use.

SUGGESTED READING

Arnheim, Rudolf. *Thoughts on Art Education*. Los Angeles: The J. Paul Getty Trust, 1989.

———.*Visual Thinking*. Berkeley and Los Angeles: The University of California Press, 1969.

Bruner, Jerome. *Child's Talk: Learning to Use Language*. New York and London: W. W. Norton and Company, 1983.

Carlsson-Paige, Nancy. *Taking Back Childhood*. New York: A Plume Book by Penguin, 2009.

Christakis, Erika. "The New Preschool Is Crushing Kids." *Atlantic*. January–February, 2016. https://www.theatlantic.com/magazine/archive/2016/01/the-new-preschool-is-crushing-kids/419139/.

Dewey, John. "My Pedagogic Creed," *School Journal* 54 (January 1897): 77–80. http://dewey.pragmatism.org/creed.htm.

Google images. https://www.google.com/imghp?hl=en&tab=wi&ei=EQm5VrvMOIjIjwP9zqywBw&ved=0EKouCBYoAQ.

Hainstock, Elizabeth G. *The Essential Montessori: An Introduction to the Woman, the Writings, the Method, and the Movement*. New York: Plume by the Penguin Group, 1978, 1986, 1997.

Housen, Abigail. *The Eye of the Beholder*. EdD diss., Harvard University Graduate School of Education, 1983.

———. "Aesthetic Thought, Critical Thinking and Transfer." *Arts and Learning Journal* 18, no. 1 (2002): 99–132.

Leeuwen, Janneke van. *The Thinking Eye: Shaping Open Minds*. London: Author, 2016. (For more information, visit www.thinkingeye.org.)

Montessori, Maria. *The Advanced Montessori Method: Spontaneous Activity in Education*, translated by Florence Simmons. New York: Frederick A. Stokes Company, 1917. https://books.google.com/books?id=UqpFAAAAIAAJ&pg=PA131&lpg=PA131&dq=#v=onepage&q&f=false.

Resnick, Lauren, and Catherine Snow. *Speaking and Listening for Preschool Through Third Grade*. Pittsburgh, PA: University of Pittsburgh Press and The National Center on Education and the Economy, 2009.

Rinaldi, Carlina. "The Relationship Between Documentation and Assess-
    ment." *Innovations in Early Education* 11, no. 1 (2004): 1–4.
Singer, Dorothy G., and Tracey A. Revenson. *A Piaget Primer: How a Child
    Thinks.* New York: A Plume Book by Penguin, 1978, 1996.
Vygotsky, Lev. *Mind in Society: The Development of Higher Psychological Pro-
    cesses.* Cambridge, MA, and London: Harvard University Press, 1978.
Yenawine, Philip. *Visual Thinking Strategies: Using Art to Deepen Learning
    Across School Disciplines.* Cambridge MA: Harvard Education Press,
    2013.
———. "Jump Starting Visual Literacy: Thoughts on Image Selection." *Art
    Education* 56, no. 1 (2003): 6–12. https://vtshome.org/publications
    -philip-yenawine/.

Two websites provide tapes of classroom discussions. The first, www
.watershed-ed.org, also has a training website and access to images for
a modest fee. The other, www.VTShome.org, has tapes and much background information and, for a subscription, provides access to images.

NOTES

Introduction

1. Diane Zimmerman (childhood speech pathologist with an emphasis on child language development, elementary principal, and superintendent), in an e-mail to the author, January 2017.
2. Francisco de Goya, *The Seesaw*, 1791–92. Oil on Canvas, 32 $^{7}/_{16}$ × 64 $^{1}/_{4}$ in. The Philadelphia Museum of Art, Gift of Miss Anna Warren Ingersoll, 1975-150-1.
3. Dori Jacobsohn (freelance VTS trainer, who for many years taught teachers-in-training in practices related to early childhood, primarily at Columbia College in Chicago), in an e-mail to the author, October 2016.
4. Philip Yenawine, *Visual Thinking Strategies: Using Art to Deepen Learning Across School Disciplines* (Cambridge, MA: Harvard Education Press, 2013).
5. Paula Lynn (museum educator on the staff of the National Gallery of Art, Washington, DC), in an e-mail to the author, July 2017.

Chapter 1

1. Dori Jacobsohn in a comment posted to her blog, *Art and Language Collaborations: Creating Language-Rich Early Childhood Environments Using Art*, January 2015, http://artandlang.com/environments-of-inquiry/.
2. Pablo Picasso, *Child with a Dove,* 1901. © 2017 Estate of Pablo Picasso/ Artists Rights Society (ARS), New York. Reproduced by permission.
3. Sarah O'Leary, transcribed from a cell phone videotape, December 2016, sent to the author, January 2017.
4. Horace Pippin, *Domino Players*, 1943. Oil on composition board, The Phillips Collection, Washington DC. ID Number: 1573. Photo credit: Reproduced by permission of Bridgeman Images.
5. Erika Miles (who teaches three- and four-year-olds at the Charlestown Nursery School in Boston) and her students, from a transcript provided to the author, February 2017.
6. Pablo Picasso, *Le Gourmet*, 1902. Oil on canvas. © Estate of Pablo Picasso/ Artists Rights Society (ARS), New York. Reproduced by permission.
7. Erika Miles, in an e-mail to the author, April 2017.

Chapter 2

1. Lauren Resnick and Catherine Snow, *Speaking and Listening for Preschool Through Third Grade* (Pittsburgh, PA: University of Pittsburgh Press and The National Center on Education and the Economy, 2009), vi.
2. Dori Jacobsohn, in an e-mail to the author, October 2016.
3. Velino Shije Herrera, *Story Teller*, ca. 1925–1935. Smithsonian American Art Museum, Washington, DC/Art Resource, New York. Reproduced by permission.
4. Diane Zimmerman, in an e-mail attachment to the author, January 2017.
5. Ibid.
6. Margaret Wise Brown and Clement Hurd, *Goodnight Moon* (New York: Harper & Row, 1947).
7. Janneke van Leeuwen, *The Thinking Eye: Shaping Open Minds* (London: Author, 2016). For more information, visit www.thinkingeye.org.
8. Rudolf Arnheim, *Visual Thinking* (Berkeley and Los Angeles: University of California Press, 1969).
9. Abigail Housen, "The Eye of the Beholder" (EdD dissertation, Harvard University Graduate School of Education, 1983).
10. Maria Izquierdo, *My Nieces (Mis Sobrinas)*, 1940. Museo Nacional de Arte Moderno, Instituto National de Bellas Artes, Mexico City, D.F., Mexico. Photo: Schalkwijk/Art Resource, NY. Reproduced by permission.
11. Fred Beaver, *Florida Seminoles Preparing Food*, 1949. National Museum of the American Indian, Smithsonian Institution, 23/8383. Photo by NMAI Photo Services. Reproduced by permission.
12. Google Images, https://www.google.com/imghp?hl=en&tab=wi&ei =EQm5VrvMOIjIjwP9zqywBw&ved=0EKouCBYoAQ. You can enter the artist and title of any images you find in this book and find links to them that you can copy and project for children to discuss. Of course, you can always search for a topic that connects particularly to your students or to what you'd like them to think about.
13. Lise White (teacher at Charlestown Nursery School, Boston, Massachusetts), in discussion with the author, March 2017.
14. Kay Cutler (director of the Fishback Center for Early Childhood Education at the University of South Dakota, Brookings), in discussion with the author, March 2017.
15. Erin Jeanneret (early childhood teacher at Mott Haven Academy, Bronx, New York), in discussion with the author, March 2017.
16. Ibid.

17. Nora Elton (mother, museum educator, art teacher, and freelance VTS teacher), in discussion with the author, March 2017.

18. Ibid.

19. White, discussion.

20. Paula Lynn, in an e-mail to the author, July 2017.

21. Sarah O'Leary, in an e-mail to the author, March 2017.

22. Dori Jacobsohn, in an e-mail to the author, February 2017.

23. "Active listening," *Wikipedia,* accessed August 22, 2017, https://en .wikipedia.org/wiki/Active_listening; "Active Listening Presentation," SlideShare, posted by "kdbourque," July 11, 2014, https://www.slideshare .net/kdbourque/active-listening-presentation-36893005.

24. Rudolf Arnheim, *Thoughts on Art Education* (Los Angeles: The J. Paul Getty Trust, 1989), 58.

25. White, discussion.

Chapter 3

1. Carly Reagan (teacher of three- and four-year-olds at Charlestown Nursery School, Boston, Massachusetts), in an e-mail to the author, April 2017.

2. Anunziata Pignatelli (preschool teacher at Public School 110 in Greenpoint, Brooklyn, New York), in discussion with the author, January 2017.

3. Erin Jeanneret (early childhood teacher at Mott Haven Academy in Bronx, New York), in discussion with the author, February 2017.

4. Lise White (teacher at Charlestown Nursery School, Boston, Massachusetts), in discussion with the author, April 2017.

5. Eric Carle, *The Very Hungry Caterpillar* (New York: Philomel Books, a division of Penguin Young Readers Group, 1969 and 1987).

6. Rosemary Agoglio (founding educator at the Eric Carle Museum of Picture Book Art), in discussion with the author and in subsequent e-mail, Spring 2017.

7. http://www.carlemuseum.org/.

8. The American Library Association's Dialogic Reading (http://www.ala.org /PrinterTemplate.cfm?section=archive&template=/ContentManagement /ContentDisplay.cfm&ContentID=43217) gives a lengthy explanation. The simplification of dialogic reading, Hear and Say Reading, is referred to at this link: https://www.ala.org/ala/alsc/ECRR/orderinginfoa /WorkshopVideos.htm.

9. Agoglio, discussion.

10. Sarah O'Leary (preschool teacher at Josiah Quincy School, Boston, Massachusetts), in discussion followed up by e-mail to the author, Winter/Spring 2017.

11. Erika Miles (preschool teacher at Charlestown Nursery School, Boston, Massachusetts), in e-mail to the author, April 2017.

12. Sarah O'Leary provided tapes of various classes in which she applied VTS with slight modifications, and all quotes are transcribed from those tapes, Spring 2017.

13. Reagan, e-mail.

14. Meg Brown (teacher of three- and four-year-olds at Charlestown Nursery School, Boston, Massachusetts), in e-mail to the author, April 2017.

15. Henri Rousseau, *Le Douanier* (*The Sleeping Gypsy*), 1897. Oil on canvas, The Museum of Modern Art, New York. Gift of Mrs. Simon Guggenheim. Digital Image © The Museum of Modern Art/Licensed by SCALA/Art Resources, New York. Reproduced by permission.

16. Dori Jacobsohn sent this transcript in an e-mail to the author, March 2017.

17. Dori Jacobsohn, in a follow-up discussion by e-mail to the author, March 2017.

Chapter 4

1. Carmen Lomas Garza, *Naranjas* (*Oranges*). © 1988 Carmen Lomas Garza. Reproduced by permission of the artist.

2. Anunziata Pignatelli (preschool teacher at Public School 110 in Greenpoint, Brooklyn, New York), who provided copies of the children's comments, which she copied down, and discussed with the author, October 2015 and January 2017.

3. Erin Jeanneret, in discussion with the author in January 2017.

4. Norah Elton, in discussion with the author, January 2017.

5. Sarah O'Leary, who provided tapes from which these comments were transcribed, Spring 2017.

6. Diego Rivera, *La Pinata* (*A Christmas Tradition*), 1953. Mural Palacio de Bellas Artes, Mexico City. Photo © 2017 Banco de México Diego Rivera Frida Kahlo Museums Trust, Mexico, D. F./Artists Rights Society (ARS), New York. Reproduced by permission.

7. O'Leary, tapes.

8. Carly Reagan (teacher of three- and four-year-olds at Charlestown Nursery School, Boston, Massachusetts), in an e-mail to the author, April 2017.

9. Lise White (teacher at Charlestown Nursery School, Boston, Massachusetts), in discussion with the author, April 2017.

10. Reagan, e-mail.

11. Erin Jeanneret (early childhood teacher at Mott Haven Academy in Bronx, New York), in discussion with the author, February 2017.

12. Anunziata Pignatelli, in discussion with the author, January 2017.

13. Ibid.

14. Kay Cutler (director of the Fishback Center for Early Childhood Education, a demonstration/laboratory nursery school at South Dakota State University in Brookings, South Dakota), in discussion with the author and by way of follow-up e-mail, Spring/Summer 2017.

15. Reagan, e-mail.

16. Erika Miles (preschool teacher at Charlestown Nursery School, Boston, Massachusetts), in e-mail with the author, April 2017.

17. O'Leary, tapes.

18. Lauren Resnick and Catherine Snow, *Speaking and Listening for Preschool Through Third Grade* (Pittsburgh, PA: University of Pittsburgh Press and The National Center on Education and the Economy, 2009), 20–21.

19. Jerome Bruner, *Child's Talk: Learning to Use Language* (New York and London: W. W. Norton and Company, 1983), 120.

20. Ibid., 39.

21. Miles, e-mail.

22. Cutler, discussion and e-mail.

23. Mary Moeller (professor on the faculty of the Teaching, Learning, and Leadership Department at South Dakota State University, Brookings, South Dakota), in discussion with the author, followed up by e-mail, March-April, 2017.

Chapter 5

1. Anna Miller (director of nursery school programs at the College of Education Early Childhood Center and the Merrill Palmer Skillman Institute Early Childhood Center at Wayne State University, Detroit, Michigan) provided the author with copies of evaluation reports done by the faculty of the centers over a three-year implementation of VTS. These are excerpts from a few; more appear later in the text. February 2017.

2. Carly Reagan (teacher of three- and four-year-olds at Charlestown Nursery School, Boston, Massachusetts), in an e-mail to the author, April 2017.

3. Two websites provide tapes of classroom discussions. The first, www .watershed-ed.org, also has a training website and access to images for a modest fee. The other, www.VTShome.org, has tapes and background information, and for a subscription, provides access to images.

4. Meg Brown (teacher of three- and four-year-olds at Charlestown Nursery School, Boston, Massachusetts), in discussion with the author, April 2017.

5. Ibid.

6. Dori Jacobsohn, in a follow-up discussion by e-mail to the author, May 2017.

7. Ibid.

8. Sarah O'Leary (preschool teacher at Josiah Quincy School, Boston, Massachusetts), in discussion followed up by e-mail with the author, Winter/Spring 2017.

9. Ibid.

10. Brown, e-mail.

11. Miller, another excerpt from an evaluation.

12. Ibid.

13. O'Leary, discussion.

14. Lise White (teacher at Charlestown Nursery School, Boston, Massachusetts), in discussion with the author, April 2017.

15. Kelly Pellagrini and Cady Audette (codirectors of the Charlestown Nursery School, Boston, Massachusetts, https://www.charlestownnursery school.org/page/about-cns). Additional information came from discussions with the author and follow-up e-mail, January–May, 2017.

Chapter 6

1. Dori Jacobsohn, in a follow-up discussion by e-mail to the author, March 2017.

2. Erika Christakis, "The New Preschool Is Crushing Kids," *Atlantic*, January–February, 2016, https://www.theatlantic.com/magazine/archive/2016/01 /the-new-preschool-is-crushing-kids/419139/.

3. Nancy Carlsson-Paige, *Taking Back Childhood* (New York: A Plume Book by Penguin, 2009), 8, 9.

4. John Dewey, "My Pedagogic Creed," *School Journal* 54 (January 1897): 77–80, http://dewey.pragmatism.org/creed.htm.

5. Ibid.

6. Ibid.

7. Dorothy G. Singer and Tracey A. Revenson, *A Piaget Primer: How a Child Thinks* (New York: A Plume Book by Penguin, 1978, 1996), 21–22.

8. Lev Vygotsky, *Mind in Society: The Development of Higher Psychological Processes* (Cambridge, MA, and London: Harvard University Press, 1978), 86.

9. Abigail Housen, "Aesthetic Thought, Critical Thinking and Transfer," *Arts and Learning Journal* 18, no. 1 (2002): 99–132.

10. Maria Montessori, *The Advanced Montessori Method: Spontaneous Activity in Education*, trans by Florence Simmons (New York: Frederick A. Stokes Company, 1917), 131, https://books.google.com/books?id=UqpFAAAAI AAJ&pg=PA131&lpg=PA131&dq=#v=onepage&q&f=false.

11. National Center for Montessori in the Public Sector, http://www.public -montessori.org.

12. Ibid.

13. Jacqueline Cossentino (Director of Research, National Center for Montessori in the Public Sector; university teacher; and occasional VTS trainer), in discussion followed up with e-mail, Spring–Summer 2017.

14. Ibid.

15. Lise White (teacher at Charlestown Nursery School, Boston, Massachusetts), in e-mail with the author, April 2017.

16. Kelly Pellagrini and Cady Audette (codirectors of the Charlestown Nursery School, Boston, Massachusetts, https://www.charlestownnursery school.org/page/about-cns). Additional information came from discussions with the author and follow-up e-mail, April–June 2017.

17. The Loris Malaguzzi International Centre website is http://www.reggio children.it/centro-internazionale-loris-malaguzzi/?lang=en.

18. Carolyn Edwards, Lella Gandini, and George Forman, eds. *The Hundred Languages of Children: The Reggio Emilia Experience in Transformation*, 3rd ed. (Santa Barbara CA: Praeger, An Imprint of ABC-CLIO, LLC, 2012).

19. Loris Malaguzzi spoke a great deal more than he wrote. This quote cannot be traced to a source, but every site that describes the Reggio Emilia Approach includes this comment. It can be found here, for example: https://www.goodreads.com/quotes/501623-stand-aside-for-a-while-and -leave-room-for-learning.

20. Carlina Rinaldi, "The Relationship Between Documentation and Assessment," *Innovations in Early Education* 11, no. 1 (2004): 3–4.

21. Jacobsohn, e-mail.

22. Anna Miller, in conversation with the author, February 2017.

23. Carlsson-Paige, *Taking Back Childhood*, 4–5.

24. Rinaldi, "The Relationship Between Documentation and Assessment," 1–2.

ACKNOWLEDGMENTS

I MUST BEGIN THESE ACKNOWLEDGMENTS with a thank you to Tad and Rebecca Yenawine, my children, for their patience and guidance as we have negotiated life together for the past half-century. My knowledge of preschoolers began as I watched them grow and both prosper and struggle. I learned from many mistakes, and as much as I regret the mistakes, I appreciate the knowledge gained. I owe them even more for introducing grandchildren into my life at particularly useful moments. As I thought more and more about early childhood education, I had Wyla Yenawine first and then Evhe Simone Carter (three-and-a-half as I write) to test every assertion. How lucky grandparents are!

My whole adventure with and commitment to VTS in preschool began because of the persistence and research abilities of the extraordinary Paula Lynn. As it will be easy to determine by reading, this book would have been impossible without the information and opportunity provided by Sarah O'Leary, who welcomed me into her classroom and sent me essential tapes to augment what I saw there; she also introduced me to Nora Elton, a great resource on teaching VTS in different settings. Dori Jacobsohn was endlessly generous, providing information about myriad subjects; unafraid to say it's not quite right yet, she kept me honest throughout. Diane Zimmerman was not only a constant source about the whole panoply of cognition involved in learning to talk and the role that images play in that development, but was also unwavering support as I struggled to write. Anna Miller, Kay Cutler, and Mary Moeller drew generously from their great stores of knowledge and experience as directors of early childhood learning centers in different cities, and they were as helpful to me as they have been to countless teachers and children. Rosemary Agoglio's great wisdom was invaluable as she counseled me on The Whole Book Approach and advised, as Dori Jacobsohn did, on the wonderful ways of the Reggio Emilia Approach to teaching and learning. Jackie Cosentino steered my further inquiry into VTS and Montessori, expanding what I knew and strengthening what I wrote.

A huge percentage of the insights and stories that enliven and give substance to this book came from the remarkable Charlestown Nursery School in Boston. Codirectors Kelly Pellagrini and Cady Audette were constantly gracious and inspiring as I sought answers to too many questions, and you have come to know their gifted, generous faculty and staff, especially Meg Brown, Erika Miles, Carly Reagan, and Lise White, truly exemplary teachers each one. Gretchen Baudenbacher introduced me to Nancy Piscatelli and her invaluable research regarding thinking and language, and Erin Jenerette, who helped me understand preschool in an intensely urban setting.

This book could not have been written without the extraordinary patience, persistence, and generosity of my editor, Nancy Walser. Her quick intelligence and her always insightful counsel are the most any author could ask for. Christopher Leonesio was the careful, attentive, and ever helpful steward of the book through production. The meticulous, helpful, kind Charles Hutchinson provided copy improvements throughout the book. The staff of the Harvard Education Press in general is always available to answer questions and provide assistance, and I want to give my heartfelt thanks to all, especially noting Douglas Clayton, Director, and Caroline Chauncey, Editor-in-Chief, who continue to believe in me and VTS.

Finally, I have no words to thank Laura Donnelley, who kept me eating while I wrote; Patricia Yenawine, who provided a sanctuary in which to write; Nick Gardner, my work partner and soul mate, who gave me time to write when he needed me for other work; Lynn Pyfer, who was ready with delightful humor as well as a commitment to bringing VTS to ever-larger numbers of teachers; Andrew Neave, who championed the effort from start to finish; and Leo Buser, whose love and caring give me inspiration and strength at every moment.

ABOUT THE AUTHOR

PHILIP YENAWINE is cocreator of Visual Thinking Strategies (VTS) with cognitive psychologist Abigail Housen. He is currently cofounder and creative director of Watershed, a nonprofit entity established to support student-centered, inquiry-based teaching, including the dissemination of VTS through an innovative online platform. Watershed forms partnerships with other organizations focused on helping reform-oriented teachers find and use resources as well as communicate with one another.

Yenawine was director of education at the Museum of Modern Art from 1983 to 1993. He also directed education programs at the Metropolitan Museum of Art and Chicago's Museum of Contemporary Art earlier in his career. He was founding director of the Aspen Art Museum and consulting curator at the Institute for Contemporary Art in Boston. He has taught art education at the School of the Art Institute in Chicago and Massachusetts College of Art. He received the National Art Education Association's Award for Distinguished Service in 1993, was the George A. Miller Visiting Scholar at the University of Illinois in 1996, and the first Educator-in-Residence at the Isabella Stewart Gardner Museum in 2012, among other honors. He is on the board of Art Matters, a foundation giving fellowships to cutting-edge artists.

Yenawine is the author of *How to Look at Modern Art*, *Key Art Terms for Beginners*, and six children's books about art among other writing projects. His most recent book, *Visual Thinking Strategies: Using Art to Deepen Learning Across School Disciplines*, was published by Harvard Education Press in October 2013. He attended Princeton University from 1960 to 1963, and holds a BA from Governor's State University, University Park, Illinois, and an MA from Goddard College, Plainfield, Vermont. He was awarded an honorary doctorate by the Kansas City Art Institute in 2003.

INDEX